positive

Surviving my bullies, finding hope,
and living to change the world

A Memoir by

PAIGE RAWL

with ALI BENJAMIN

HARPER

An Imprint of HarperCollins*Publishers*

Library of Congress Cataloging-in-Publication Data

Rawl, Paige.

Positive : surviving my bullies, finding hope, and living to change the
world : a memoir / by Paige Rawl with Ali Benjamin. — First edition.

pages cm

ISBN 978-0-06-234251-5 (hardback)

1. Rawl, Paige—Health. 2. HIV-positive children—Biography.
3. AIDS (Disease) in adolescence—Patients—Biography. 4. AIDS (Disease)
in adolescence—Social aspects. 5. Bullying—Psychological aspects.
I. Benjamin, Ali. II. Title.

RJ387.A25R38 2014   2014005857

362.19697'9200835—dc23   CIP

                                                               AC

Typography by Sarah Creech

14 15 16 17 18   CG/RRDH   10 9 8 7 6 5 4 3 2 1

First Edition

+   +   +

*For my mom, who has always been my rock
and believed in me. I couldn't have
made it without you. I love you!*

*To the memory of my dad,
Charles Newman Rawl II.*

*For anyone who has ever been bullied or
stigmatized—don't give up on yourself.*

+   +   +

+ FOREWORD +

by Jay Asher

When you open a book about someone's life, written by that person, you don't expect the first words to be written by someone else. So you may be wondering, *What's* this *guy doing here?*

Well, it might help to think of this less as a book and more as a powerful conversation you're about to have with someone. Maybe you've heard a little about that person, and you're drawn to know more. If you saw that person walking down a sidewalk or at a party, the most comfortable way to start that conversation is to be introduced.

Reader, I would love you to meet Paige Rawl. When you two have finished talking, I think you're going to walk away a new person.

At the end of the book are a few pages filled with information about important issues—bullying, HIV/AIDS, and suicide. (Their statistics may surprise you, which highlights our need to make sure people know more about them.) There are also resources and ways you can help people dealing with these issues. Or maybe help yourself. Knowing more about these topics can, at the very least, make life better for a lot of people. At most, it can save a life.

But in between this introduction and those pages, you'll meet Paige. She will tell you, in vivid, captivating detail, her story—and it's a roller-coaster ride of emotion. It moves from heartbreaking to heartwarming, and will move *you* from feeling infuriated to uplifted and inspired.

Thirteen Reasons Why, my novel about a teenage girl who commits suicide, but only after making a set of audio recordings to describe her reasons why, was prompted by a personal experience. My character is fictional, but my understanding of that deep despair came from conversations with a relative who attempted suicide as a teen.

I believe life always leaves opportunities for hope, but through those conversations I understood how someone could give up looking for it—how even hoping for hope could be painful.

Over the years, countless people have explained to me the different ways my book has affected them. It reminded them of the ways, good and bad, big and small, that we each affect one another every day. It showed them that we never fully know what someone else is struggling with. And it encouraged people to fight for the help and respect they deserve.

Storytelling does that. It lets us see the world from someone else's perspective. It lets us explore issues from a safe distance because they're not happening to us—not in that precise way. We can judge a character's emotions and decisions, weighing them against our own. We can decide not to become like one character, or try to be more like another.

But when the story is true, as it is in *Positive*, that safe distance can waver—perhaps feeling uncomfortably close. ("I've never behaved like *that* person, have I?") It can lead us to ponder questions that are important yet difficult to ask on our own. And when a story does that, it changes the way we see everything, including ourselves.

Sometimes in life we get introduced to a person who helps us ask those questions. That person may be knocked down and held down for so long that she breaks. She shatters. But given a second chance, she chooses to rise higher than she ever thought possible. And she chooses to use her life's experiences to bring the people she meets up with her.

And when, let's say, she writes a book about those experiences, we're *all* invited to rise with her.

That is why it is my great honor to introduce you to Paige Rawl, who I first met within the very words now placed in your hands. Once she tells you her story—once you read her truth—I know you will become fast friends and feel thoroughly inspired, just as I have.

Author's Note

We all have our own truths. Together our truths form the human experience.

Surely, everyone in the pages that follow—friends and not-friends—have their truths to tell. Some people who I've depicted will barely recognize themselves; others don't know and might never have guessed how they affected me.

Certainly, there are plenty of people whose stories intersect with mine, and whose truths I never got to know.

I'll simply say this: while the names of many people and places have been changed—including the name of my middle school—the characters in this book are real people whose lives touched my own.

The sole exceptions are the kids I describe having met in the stress center. The real-life kids I met during my brief hospitalization can decide to share their particular stories, if they wish. But in the meantime, their literary equivalents are based on many I have met along this journey—real kids who shared with me their worries and fears, stresses and sorrows.

The pain of all those stories is real enough.

Otherwise, what follows in these pages is the truth of the world, as I remember it.

Preface

Nobody quite prepares you for the moment you see your own name scrawled on a bathroom wall.

To be honest, until I saw my own name, it never really occurred to me that all those names I'd seen before—all those names that appeared on the restroom walls of Dunkin' Donuts and 7-Elevens, the Castleton Square Mall and the corner gas station—represented actual human beings.

If I ever bothered to wonder about those people, even briefly—*Will Jasmyn actually love Shawn 4ever? What happened to Darren that we should never, ever forget him?*—the moment surely would have passed long before I washed my hands and placed them beneath the whirring hand dryer.

Then one day, I walked into a bathroom in my middle school, and there was my name in thick black marker. Beneath it, other kids had added their own words in ballpoint pen.

I never in a million years expected to see my name on this wall. I'd always considered myself a good girl—more *Glee* than *Kardashians*, more Taylor Swift than Miley Cyrus. I was born a joiner, not a fighter.

But I was beginning to realize that sometimes a person doesn't get to choose whether she joins or fights. Sometimes the joining is impossible, sometimes the fight chooses you. The universe plucks you—you, specifically—out of all those souls out there and hands you something that makes fitting in and going with the flow utterly out of the question.

"I'm sorry," the universe says. "I'm afraid you're going to have to fight."

And when you stare back at the universe, not understanding, it simply shrugs. "You'd better start now. Or this world will destroy you."

I didn't have a choice: I had to learn to fight.

As my story unfolded over the next few years, I'd learn some things. I'd learn that you can fight with a smile. That you can fight in a dress, or a cheerleader's skirt, pom-poms in hand. You can even fight just by wearing a sparkling tiara and a satin sash that says MISS INDIANA HIGH SCHOOL AMERICA.

But I hadn't figured those things out just yet. All I knew, standing in the girls' room, was that everything I knew, everything I had planned for myself, was changing.

I stared at the writing and considered my options.

I could scribble it all out, just try to erase the whole thing. Unfortunately, the only writing utensil in my purse was a pen. It might cross out those added comments, but it would never, ever cover that fat black marker.

Besides, crossing out the words wouldn't stop people from thinking things about me. It wouldn't change anyone's mind.

There was nothing to do. Nothing to do but look in the mirror and smooth down my hair, take a deep breath, and push the door open. By the time I stepped into the hallway I was smiling, as if I hadn't seen a thing, as if all was exactly as it should be. As if that felt-tipped warning to all the other kids, that I didn't belong—that I was to be shamed and shunned— never existed.

PAIGE HAS AIDS, it read.

Then underneath—*Slut. Whore.*

And finally, *PAIGE=PAIDS.*

Actually, I had HIV, not AIDS. They're related, but they're

not the same thing—not that the facts mattered to the kids at Clarkstown Middle School.

Just like it didn't matter that I wasn't contagious, that HIV wasn't like a cold or flu, that I posed no risk to them whatsoever.

Nor did it matter that there was nothing visible about my virus, that I looked and walked and talked exactly and completely like everyone else. It didn't even matter that the kids who were giving me the hardest time had been my friends, my good friends, just last year.

You know how it is: I had something that others didn't have. I was different.

And I was learning that when you live in a suburban neighborhood on the northwest side of Indianapolis, and you are in seventh grade, and all you want is to be surrounded by friends, *different* is about the very worst thing you can be.

+ CONTENTS +

Part Three: Falling

Part Four: Becoming

PART ONE

Beginning

What Was

Today, when I tell people that I took medicine every single day for almost a decade without ever once wondering why, they sometimes look at me like I have three heads. Or maybe like I'm the world's biggest idiot.

I can see their point.

But from my earliest memories, the medicine has just been a part of my life.

There I am as a very young child, scrambling up onto the kitchen counter, folding my legs *crisscross-applesauce*, and waiting patiently. And there is my mother, twisting the child safety lid off a white plastic jar, scooping a heap of powder, and stirring it, still lumpy, into a plastic sippy cup filled with milk.

She places the lid on the cup and hands it to me. I make a face and begin to drink. The taste is awful; I call this drink "my yucky." Still, I'm a dutiful child: I drink it all. I would have, every time, even if my mother hadn't been watching me closely, her eyes focused on this ritual as if my life depended on it.

It did, of course, although I didn't know that yet.

Other times, people ask about my hospital visits. There had to have been so many. Did I really think that was normal? The short answer is, yes. I did. Not only that, I *liked* it.

The Riley Hospital for Children is located in downtown Indianapolis. Its vast modern architecture and the hustle and bustle of the city around it seemed such an exciting contrast to our cozy one-story ranch home with its tidy patch of cut grass. Inside the hospital entrance, I looked up. All around the atrium I would see enormous teddy bears perched on beams high overhead, their legs dangling. I'd pass a shiny carousel horse surrounded by pennies; each time, my mother and I both made wishes and tossed our own coins toward the animal. I'd wish for dolls and dresses, for trips to the water park, for cupcakes and Christmas. My mother made her wish silently.

When I asked what she wished for, she never told me. Instead, she would simply answer, "Same as last time, pumpkin." She'd hug me close, then, and finish, ". . . Same as every time."

We'd step into the glass elevators, real glass elevators, just like Willy Wonka's, and rise to the third floor.

Waiting in the doctor's office, I could never keep myself from touching the medical equipment. I squeezed the rubber blood pressure pump, slipped the plastic caps on and off of the otoscope, pulled down on the rubbery black coils that connected these tools to the wall.

"Stop messing with the doctor's stuff," my mom would always try to scold me, unable to completely hide the hint of a smile on her face. "She's going to get mad at you, Paige!" But when Dr. Cox at last breezed into the room, in her funky shoes and chunky jewelry, she was never angry. Instead, she greeted me cheerfully.

"Paige! It's good to see you!" Her flowing, loose-fitting clothes peeked out from beneath her lab coat. Her stethoscope hung confidently around her neck.

I loved seeing her. One day, I planned to *be* her.

"I'm going to have your job when I grow up," I would announce proudly at my visits.

"I know you will." Dr. Cox would smile back, brushing a streak of blond hair from her eyes and holding out a tongue depressor. She always took me seriously, not the way some grown-ups treat kids.

She would press the wooden depressor on my tongue. "Now say *ahh*."

I told Dr. Cox everything. About school, and sleepovers with my friends, that I swam like a mermaid, which I knew because my mother said it was true. I told her I loved karaoke and that I could jump high as the birds on my trampoline. She listened and laughed, complimented my sparkly nails. She asked about my vacations, teachers, classmates. . . .

I may have been her patient, just a young child, but Dr. Cox treated me like a real person, someone she genuinely liked. She wasn't the only one. The nurses in the emergency room knew me by name, remembered details about both my health history and my life outside the hospital. They asked me about books I was reading, they cheered when I told them I'd learned to ride a bike. The lab technicians knew me, too—they asked me about school as they pricked my skin, distracting me by allowing me to hold the tubes that were filling up with my blood.

Being at a hospital so regularly, so young, sounds awful to folks who have no experience inside a place like Riley. But the truth is, I can think of far worse fates than to have a group of people this warm, this kind, be a part of your life from the start.

And when these things—the medicine, the hospital visits—become part of your routine before you even form your first memory—before you write your name for the first time, before you can skip, or turn a somersault, or even brush your teeth without assistance, the whole thing becomes a bit like the sun rising. If it somehow *didn't* happen—if one morning the darkness never gave way to light, if the stars remained overhead even as the morning school bus lurched up to the corner and opened its doors for its line of bewildered kids—now *that* would get your attention. But as long as it happens, day after day without ever taking a break, you start to take the whole thing for granted. Your mind wanders to other things, like finishing your homework or an upcoming vocabulary test or last weekend's sleepover.

Take it from me: the things that keep you alive can be like the hum of the refrigerator, or the television that your mom leaves on all day because she gets nervous when there's too much quiet.

They're just there, just a part of your world, barely even worth a mention.

Perhaps you think it would have been different for you— that you would wonder sooner, that you would clue in earlier that *something is different here.* You would have started asking questions, all those *what/why/hows.*

I'll be honest: I'm not so sure about that.

And maybe that was my problem from the start—the fact that those thousands of doses of medicine had been so routine, so humdrum. Bitter-tasting, sure. A bummer, I guess. But still just a backdrop to the parts of my life that felt like they really mattered. Perhaps *that* was the reason everything that happened later was such a surprise to me. Maybe, in the end, it was the very regularity of it that left me so unprepared when it all went so badly.

And that's how it was, year after year. My friend Azra went to her grandmother's to swim in her pool. My friend Jasmine went to her brother's baseball games. I went to see Dr. Cox. I took medicine and played soccer and dressed my Barbies and sang country songs with my mother and watched my crimson blood flow into clear plastic tubes.

It was just what I *did.* Nothing more.

I had plenty of friends, and it was, to be honest, a pretty good life.

Mom

For my mother, of course, the hospital experience was completely different.

For one thing, she knew why we were there.

Mom knew that for all of their cheerfulness, those nurses and doctors and lab techs were actually engaged in a life-and-death battle—a fight for my young life. My mom knew that deep inside my cells, a tiny virus, a million times smaller than the period at the end of this sentence, was trying to kill me.

Here is the thing, the very simple reason I have any sort of story to tell: years ago, probably before I was even born, the human immunodeficiency virus, HIV, invaded my immune system, inserting its own genetic blueprint into the very cells that were supposed to keep me healthy. Every time my own cells divided, the virus replicated, too.

My mom also knew that if it were left unchecked, the HIV virus would turn into AIDS, a disease for which there is no cure. She knew that if that happened, I would be unable to fight even the simplest infections; every system in my body would be ravaged by other viruses and bacteria, by fungal infections, by parasites. Even the common cold would become life threatening. Eventually, I would get an infection that I couldn't survive.

My mom knew that by the time we met Dr. Cox, AIDS had already killed over eleven million people worldwide, including nearly three million children.

My mother knew all of these things. She couldn't help but know.

And while doctors' visits and medicines have always just been there in my own memory—a part of my world for as long as I could remember—my mother's own journey had a very specific beginning.

For her, there was a before, then an after.

My parents at their wedding.

Mom had grown up on the north side of Indianapolis, just a stone's throw from the clean lawns and limestone buildings of Butler University. The daughter of a contractor and homemaker, her childhood had been a safe, rather ordinary one, punctuated by the occasional Baptist church service or neighborhood baseball game. She met my dad when she was in her twenties—she was a bartender, and he came in for a drink. He was a former navy officer, the son of a military man. He owned a used car lot and had the friendly charm, the charisma, that makes an outstanding salesman. They talked. He made her laugh. They discovered that they each loved boating and country music.

I think about this now, think about them young and free, sitting in a bar and laughing together. I guess it is always weird to think about your parents young and happy, at the start of a relationship that hasn't had the chance to see any struggle or grow old. But trust me: it is even weirder when one of them has since given the other one HIV, changing everyone's life, and future generations, forever.

He seemed like such a nice guy, she says. People always say that, don't they? They say it later, after the fact. After the person has done something unforgivable. *Such a nice guy. Funny. Never would have seen it coming.*

They went boating together in Morse Lake and talked some more. He told her he wanted a child. He thought it might be fun to coach Little League someday. And with the wind blowing through her hair, the sun reflecting on the water around them, she dared to imagine a life with him. She grinned at the thought: this handsome man, her husband, coaching a child—their child. She wanted that. She wanted to stand in the bleachers and cheer.

She wanted *him*.

After they married, my mom helped out at the car lot, answering phones when my dad went to automobile auctions to buy new inventory. Then they had a baby girl together: me.

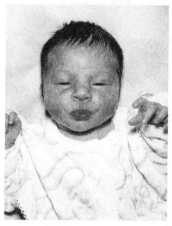

Brand-new me! August 11, 1994.

By then, the business was doing well. They were earning money—more money than Mom expected.

Who knows, maybe that money was the problem.

Dad started getting jealous, accusing my mom of things she never did, of relationships she never had. No amount of assurance could convince him. He had severe ups and downs, and his behavior became erratic. Money disappeared, and sometimes my father didn't come home for several days.

He did some stints in rehab. The car business suffered. My mother learned he had been cheating on her. They split up, then got back together. She cried, and he made promises he didn't keep. Eventually, they broke apart for good.

I don't remember any of this, of course. Nor do I remember some of the other things my mom has told me: about how I slept well and laughed often. About learning to talk—my first word was "Dada"—then walk, then run.

My first "modeling gig," sitting in a flashy new car at my parents' lot.

Mom says she used to hold me at the window in the afternoons. I was fascinated by the yellow school buses that rumbled past, filled with big kids. I squealed with laughter as they passed. Waiting for them, watching them, became a happy ritual for us.

Then came her fevers.

My mother thought perhaps she had the flu. Her body ached, and she felt weak. She couldn't get warm, yet she broke into sweats. The symptoms were mild at first—she was still diapering me and chasing me, strapping me into my car seat and folding piles of laundry—but she just couldn't seem to shake this thing, whatever it was.

She visited her doctor a few times. He recommended blood work. They discussed anemia, chronic fatigue.

On the day she came in for her follow-up visit, HIV was the last thing on her mind. After all, she was a Midwestern mother, living in the suburbs. Her life revolved around work and breakfast cereals, around pouring laundry detergent and picking up toys and making beds.

Sure, my dad had struggled. But *she* hadn't. So she was totally unprepared for the news the doctor delivered.

"Your blood test results came back," he said. She tells me his voice was very matter-of-fact. "You are HIV positive."

My mom helping me dye Easter eggs. At this point,
she was still unaware of our HIV status.

. . .

I don't know what those early days after the diagnosis would have been like for her—even now, all these years later, she finds it difficult talking about that time. She tells me that she called her own mother and sobbed into the phone. That her sister drove down from Wisconsin, and she sobbed onto her sister's shoulder. That she called my father, the only one who could have possibly given her the infection, and sobbed as she told him he needed an HIV test.

She tells me something else: that she was terrified she would leave me motherless. I was two and a half at the time.

And then there came another thought.

Mothers can pass the disease to babies during pregnancy or birth. What if I also . . .

No way, my mother reassured herself. I couldn't possibly have HIV. After all, I was fat and happy, developing normally. My only health problems had been a couple of routine earaches.

But still. The thought lingered with my mother. What if I was HIV positive, too?

In midsummer, just before my third birthday, Mom brought me to the pediatrician's office. There, she held me as a technician drew blood from my chubby little arm. Two weeks went by before she called the doctor's office for the results.

The doctor told her right then, over the phone: I, too, had tested positive for HIV.

She sank down into a chair and started shaking.

Her daughter, her beloved toddler with the pudgy cheeks and the tiny hands stretched toward her in a hug, was infected with a virus that had already killed tens of millions of people—a virus for which there was no cure.

That afternoon, she held me at the window as usual, and I squealed with delight, as usual, when the school buses passed.

She kissed the top of my head and held me tightly and tried to fight back the tears that wouldn't stop coming.

It was those big yellow school buses that got her, she said. She wondered if I would ever get to ride one.

My third birthday. My mom had learned my HIV status just weeks earlier.

Clarkstown

*2006 was an important year. I was excited to start
middle school—and would soon find out about my diagnosis.*

On my first day of sixth grade, I was completely and totally
giddy. My mom, on the other hand, was a nervous wreck.

"Hurry, Paige," she shouted from the kitchen. She has a
funny way of getting loud when she is stressed out. On this
morning, she was so loud that I cringed, even though I was
two rooms away, getting ready in the bathroom. "If you don't
have breakfast, you might pass out."

I rolled my eyes at my own reflection in the mirror. I knew
that wasn't true, I wasn't going to pass out, just as I knew that
I had plenty of time for a decent breakfast.

But I also knew my mother.

Through all of elementary school, Mom had insisted on being right there with me—she was a constant chaperone at field trips, a front-row attendee at plays and concerts. She was the parent who planned the classroom parties, who doled out cupcakes and served Dixie Cups of apple juice, who handed out napkins with little squares of brownie, or a tiny handful of potato chips. Every Halloween, she gave each child in my class a small pumpkin to decorate and a plastic bag filled with toys and treats.

She just felt more comfortable when she was by my side—exactly by my side.

But now I was starting Clarkstown Middle School, and she was a mess.

"You know, Mom," I called out, "*you* went to Clarkstown and it was just fine."

"I know, Paige," she answered back. "But times are different now. The world's gone all crazy."

"And your old gym teacher is still there. She's one of the school counselors, so I'll probably see her lots."

I heard a drawer open and shut, the sound of running water in the kitchen.

"You better not," my mother called. "These days, it's mostly the bad kids who see counselors. They don't have any time for the good kids."

I shook my head. My mom could be so loony tunes sometimes.

"Jeez, Mom. I'll just be a few blocks down the road. You could practically throw a stone and hit the school."

"I'm not going to be throwing anything anywhere," she said. She stepped into the bathroom and handed me a glass of Carnation Instant Breakfast, the drink she has given to me every morning for as long as I can remember. "Here," she said.

I put down the hairbrush and took as many gulps as I could.

I figured I could do at least this much for her. If I didn't have a big breakfast—this drink before my medicine, a bowl of cereal after—she would be a wreck all morning.

My mom. She gets so nervous, even today.

Mom stepped back and surveyed my outfit. "You look cute," she said, her voice a little softer this time. "I like those shorts."

"No more uniforms!" I cheered.

"No more uniforms," she repeated, a little less enthusiastic than I.

"Yay, Wildcats!"

"Yay, Wildcats," she said with a sigh. She shook her head. But she smiled, too. "I'm glad you're excited about middle school."

I took a huge slurp of my drink and set it down on the counter. Then I jumped into a cheerleading-ready position, and went through some of the basic motions—T motion, broken T, touchdown.

"Wildcats, Wildcats, go, go, go!"

I ended with my arms in a V, high above my head.

Clarkstown had a cheerleading team, and even though I couldn't join it until next year, I was already practicing. I was determined to know every routine, all the moves, before sixth grade was even finished.

"Okay, pumpkin," Mom said. "Medicine."

I followed her into the kitchen, bouncing all the while. She handed me my dose.

By now, I was old enough to take pills. I held one of the pills up. It was enormous—nearly the size of a dime. "Think about it this way, Mom," I said. "How many kids do you know who can swallow pills this size?" I held one up, as if she had never seen them before, as if she hadn't seen them every day for the last nine years. "I mean, if I can handle these, I can handle middle school. Right?"

She watched as I swallowed, making sure that I took them exactly as directed. Only when I opened my mouth to show her that the pills were gone did she grin.

"Yeah, you can, Paige," she said. "I know you can."

The Short-As-Possible Explanation of HIV

Those medicines, by the way, are the very reason I was still around.

I got lucky, you see. Like, insanely, pennies-from-heaven, four-leaf-clover-on-a-rabbit's-foot kind of lucky. That's because the year before I was diagnosed with HIV—the *very* year before—the first of those medicines came on the market.

Had I not gotten so lucky, had I been born just a few years earlier, I'd be dead by now. I'm not being dramatic when I say that, not trying to get your attention with what my English teacher would call "hyperbole." I'm just stating a fact.

Those medicines changed everything.

HIV is a virus. Viruses are funny things—everyone thinks of them as living things, but they aren't. Not really. They can't grow or reproduce on their own. But when they invade living cells, they *behave* like living things. They hijack those cells to make copies of themselves. So, in a way, it could be said that viruses borrow life—or steal it.

If you're infected by bacteria—which are alive—you can take antibiotics to kill them. But if you have a virus—be it the flu, or the common cold, or HIV—there's nothing to kill, because that virus was never alive in the first place.

With most viruses, your own body eventually produces, all on its own, everything you need to fight them off. Special cells in your body—among them, white blood cells—are constantly on the lookout for viruses and other invaders that can make you sick. They're like the friendly neighborhood cops walking a regular beat, just keeping their eye out for something that might be amiss. If they detect something in your body that doesn't belong—a virus, a bacteria, a fungus, or a parasite—these cells snap to attention. They band together, form a miniature army, and go rushing off to fight the intruder. Sometimes the cells make antibodies that overpower the infection. Other times, they swarm and devour the infection like a pack of hungry dogs. Whatever they do, those germ-fighting cells—those cops who can recognize and destroy an invader—are called your immune system. It's what allows you to get better when you catch a cold or flu.

This type of war is going on inside everyone, every single second of their lives. It's going on inside you right now. At this very instant, as you read these words, your body is being bombarded by germs, and your immune system is fighting them. It doesn't matter that you're not aware of it—it's happening. Most of the time, it works brilliantly well.

But HIV is like the evil genius of viruses. HIV turns your immune system on itself.

An HIV virus looks like a tiny ball, covered in seventy-two spikes. Picture a burr that might attach itself to your sweater during a walk in the autumn woods, or one of those medieval weapons with spikes. HIV looks like a miniature version of those things. It's big for a virus, at four-millionths of an inch, but it's still so small it can't even be seen with most microscopes.

As tiny as it is, the virus is as powerful as anything you will ever encounter.

HIV invades a special type of white blood cell, called a CD4 cell, or T-cell. Once inside that cell, HIV, that evil genius, turns the cell into a miniature HIV factory. The cell stops fighting invaders to keep you healthy, and instead churns out more and more copies of HIV.

The virus quickly spreads through the whole body that way, attacking one T-cell after another, turning each from a good-guy disease fighter into a bad-guy HIV factory.

When enough T-cells have been damaged that way, the immune system becomes too weak to fight infections.

Healthy people have about seven hundred to a thousand T-cells in a single drop of blood. Most people with HIV have fewer. If a person with HIV has five hundred or more T-cells in that amount, they're considered operating at "normal" levels. But if their T-cell counts (also called CD4 counts) fall below two hundred, that person can no longer fight infections effectively. At that point, the person has AIDS—acquired immune deficiency syndrome. *Acquired*, because they got it from an infection. *Immune deficiency*, because the part of their body that fights infection is weak. *Syndrome*, because it's a group of health problems that collectively make up a disease.

In other words, it's not HIV that kills people. It's that HIV destroys the very parts of you that would otherwise keep you strong. It makes your immune system so weak you can't fight germs, putting you at risk for diseases that most people, noninfected people, rarely have to think about.

Oh, and you know one of the most evil genius–like things about HIV? A person can be infected for years—decades, even—before they show any signs. They look and feel totally and completely normal—so normal that a drug user might want to share a needle with them, say. Or someone might not think twice about sleeping with them without using protection.

Or a mother—like my own—might get pregnant, having no idea that there's a virus inside her, one that's passing from her blood right into her infant's.

Which is exactly how the infection has been passed on, year after year after year.

So, let's say I had been less fortunate. Let's say I had been born even a few years earlier. Here's how it would have gone for me:

My T-cells would have started making more and more copies of the HIV virus. Each of those viruses would invade other cells, which in turn would make even more viruses. I'd look and feel normal for a while, then eventually I'd start getting weird infections, the type that pose no threat to a healthy person. They would come at me one after another— meningitis, pneumonia, tuberculosis, thrush, bronchitis, CMV retinitis, lymphoma, toxoplasmosis, encephalopathy, esophagitis, Kaposi's sarcoma—I could catch any of them along with a whole host of other things that are every bit as horrible as they sound.

Eventually, one of them would have killed me.

But the medicine I take each morning keeps the HIV virus from making copies of itself inside my cells. If HIV turns immune cells into an HIV factory, these medications essentially "turn off" the factory's assembly line. They stop HIV production in its tracks.

Take that, evil genius.

These treatments aren't cures. At this point in time, there is no cure; once HIV is in your body, it's there forever. But by stopping the factory, the medicine makes it possible to live with HIV for a long, long time. Possibly indefinitely.

I'll be the first to tell you that there are some challenges with these treatments: it's easy for HIV to develop resistance to the drugs, so you must use multiple drugs at the same time, and it's essential that the drugs be given every single day, at the exact same time every day. No exceptions. That's why my mother was always so vigilant about me taking my "yucky," why she always watched me until every bit of the medicine was consumed.

It's not much fun to take these medicines, either. They can cause a bunch of nasty side effects. Patients get dizzy and tired (I sure do). Their skin can turn colors, and they are constantly dealing with stomach upsets (no skin changes here, but stomach upsets are an everyday matter). And I have read on the package insert that sometimes patients can't sleep, or they get depressed. Sometimes they even hallucinate. I looked that word up the first time I read it, *hallucinate*, and I was glad that it hadn't happened to me, because frankly *seeing things that weren't there* sounded pretty scary.

Still, the people who take these drugs are alive. I am alive.

I lived until three years old, because I got lucky. But since my diagnosis, I've stayed alive thanks to two things: first is a series of astounding medical breakthroughs, a brilliant understanding among scientists of complicated processes that happen deep inside a cell.

The second is the vigilance of my mother, who never once let me miss a dose of medicine, who watched over me with concern that I swear was second to no other parent on Earth.

Her worry, her anxiety, her relentless and fierce determination to protect me: these things have literally saved my life.

I'm telling you: face-to-face with my mom, even an evil genius doesn't stand a chance.

Clarkstown

I loved Clarkstown Middle School the moment I pushed open the glass front doors.

The building was a riot of noise and energy, kids calling out to one another across the hall, waving and laughing. Overhead, flags draped down from the ceiling, flags of every country, every color. All around me were kids who seemed like the living embodiment of those flags. They were from so many different backgrounds it was almost dizzying—there were blond ponytails and beaded cornrows and silky head scarves all around me, in equal measure.

I tightened the straps of my backpack—it was so heavy with all of these middle school notebooks and binders. I lifted my chin a little higher and followed directions to the sixth-grade lockers.

And, seriously: those lockers! It may be silly, but I adored them. I loved having a locker, loved the sound of it slamming shut, loved decorating the inside with photos of friends and cutout words from magazines.

I loved other things about Clarkstown, too. I loved that it had a football field in back, with a giant scoreboard towering over the field. The field was bordered by a track, a real track with lines dividing different lanes, just like you'd find in a high school. I planned to run track this year—it was one of the few sports that sixth graders could join—and then next year stand on that track in a cheerleading uniform. I imagined myself shaking pom-poms toward the metal bleachers as a football team collided dramatically behind me. I had everything I needed to be a great cheerleader, I was sure of it. People always told me how energetic I was, that my energy was *infectious*. (Yes, that is a word they actually used from time to time.)

I loved sharing my enthusiasm, my *infectious energy*, with a group of people. Plus, I was small enough to climb easily to the top of a pyramid, so that would help.

I loved that Clarkstown had tennis courts, and a case full of trophies outside the gym, and more activities to choose from than I could have possibly participated in. I loved that we were going to get to have real dances, and also lock-ins, which were like giant slumber parties at the school where no one sleeps. I loved that there were so many kids I didn't yet know. Many different elementary schools fed into Clarkstown, which meant that all around me were faces I didn't recognize, new kids to meet.

Every one of those kids, I imagined, was a potential new friend.

On that first morning at Clarkstown, the entire sixth grade— there were so many of us now!—filed into the auditorium for an assembly. On the stage in front of us stood a short woman with extremely white hair. She wore a tight, boxy suit, and she looked a bit like a Lego person—wide and square. She teetered precariously on pumps. She broke out into an enormous smile. All of us, some three hundred kids, shifted in our seats.

"Welcome, everyone," she said. "I am Norma Fischer, the very proud principal of Clarkstown Middle School."

From behind me, I heard someone whisper loudly, "She looks like a marshmallow." A bunch of kids around me started laughing. I began to giggle, too.

A few rows ahead of me, a girl whipped around. She had dark hair, the color of Coca-Cola, and eyes to match. She shot a withering look at the boy who whispered. Then she turned back to Miss Fischer, her back straight.

I quickly looked down and stopped myself from laughing. That girl had snapped me back to attention. I never got in trouble in elementary school, and I didn't plan to start now.

If the very proud principal of Clarkstown Middle School noticed us laughing, she didn't show it. "I like to say," she continued, "that when you come to Clarkstown, you come as you are . . . and leave different."

She spoke to us about rules and expectations, about how privilege comes only with responsibility. She said that middle school was going to be more challenging and more fun than we'd imagined, that great opportunities awaited us.

As she spoke, I glanced around the room, studying some of the new faces. After a while, I stopped listening to Miss Fischer at all. How was I supposed to pay attention to all those rules right now, when I just couldn't wait to start meeting people? I looked at one kid after another, kids of every size and shape.

Sixth grade was a funny age. Some of these kids still looked like they belonged in elementary school—short, skinny limbs, and loose-fitting clothes. Others looked like teenagers already.

I realized that by the time we leave, we would all look like— we would all actually *be*—teenagers.

Come as you are, and leave different.

I glanced again at the girl with dark eyes. There was something about her, something I liked. She looked smart and practical and reliable. At the same time, though, I'd seen an intensity in those eyes. She looked like the kind of girl who would know exactly how to power her way into becoming a teenager.

I decided right then that I wanted to be her friend.

Miss Fischer introduced some of the other administrators to the students, told us where to go when we had problems. She told us that they—the staff and teachers and counselors and administrators alike—were there for us. Then she smiled at us, warmly, and sent us off to our classes.

We spilled out of the auditorium, a river of movement, of chatter and laughter and denim and hoodies and Pacers T-shirts.

We scooted off to classes, learned how to get to the gym, to the orchestra room, to the library. There were more textbooks and notebooks than I had ever had before, and I realized that Miss Fischer was right—it was going to get more challenging, what with science labs and typed book reports and algebraic equations.

Between classes, I noticed the dark-haired girl again. She carried a musical instrument in a case—a violin, maybe. She must have sensed me looking, because she looked up, right at me. Our eyes locked, and I smiled. She waited a moment, eyeing me cautiously. Then one corner of her mouth turned up, almost imperceptibly.

Oh, God, it was all so much fun, like a whole new world was opening up for me. For all of us.

That was the thing—I was twelve years old, almost a teenager, and everything in my life, everything around me, was brimming with possibility.

The Brochure

You know how people say that things happen for a reason? I believe it.

The best gifts seem to come out of the blue, no explanation. They look random—often they don't even look like gifts at all. You pick them up, though, because they are the things that happen to be in front of you.

You take a chance.

Then years later, when you trace back your own steps, you realize that this thing was *it*, that this moment was the fork in the road, the one thing that changed everything. And you didn't even know it.

You hear it all the time: a missed train connection. A bummer at first, until the person realizes that his wallet was in the car in the parking lot and the lights had been left on. Or better yet: he has a random conversation with a stranger while waiting for the next train. Fifty years later, you've got a couple about to celebrate their golden anniversary. Three kids. Eight grandkids.

That sort of thing.

Or maybe the whole reason you can speak in front of people, feel comfortable getting up and saying something with conviction, all comes down to the fact that one day, back when you were a kid, you walked into the kitchen and saw something that had been mailed to you at random.

For me, it was a brochure.

. . .

I was eight years old when I saw it sitting on the kitchen counter: a colorful brochure, vibrant among stacks of bills and boring grown-up mail.

On the cover, I saw a photo of a girl in a glittery gown, a dazzling crown on her head. I picked it up: it was an invitation to participate in something called a Sweetheart pageant.

They were asking *me* to take part.

I swear I thought my heart would burst. I'd been watching pageants with my mom ever since I could remember. I'd gazed enviously at every pageant queen that I'd ever seen in a parade—watched them wave to the crowd like they were real-life princesses. My favorite game was dressing up, wrapping myself in my mom's scarves as if I, too, were a sash-wearing pageant queen. Now here was my chance: a real pageant, and they wanted me!

Okay, so looking back I realize now that they probably sent that brochure to every girl my age in Indiana. But I didn't understand that then; I thought they really and truly wanted *me*.

I ran to my mom's room and thrust the brochure at her. I was completely breathless. "Please, Mom," I begged. "Please, please, please."

I was so sure she would say yes. She'd never been like other mothers that way. Other mothers almost always start with no. *No, you can't have cookies for snack. No, I can't take you to the park. No, I don't have time to be a customer in your pretend restaurant.*

But not my mother. My mom's first instinct has always been yes. *Yes* to the cookies, *yes* to the park, *yes* to being a restaurant customer, and *why yes, of course, I would like another heaping serving of string spaghetti*. Her yes is why all my friends love her. It is why they want to be here, at my house, for playdates. And it is why, standing there in her bedroom, brochure in my hand,

I was 100 percent certain she would let me do this pageant.

But instead, Mom just frowned. She was silent for a few moments as she looked through the brochure carefully. Then she handed it back to me and shook her head. "I don't know, honey."

I looked down at the brochure in my hands. The girl's hair cascaded around her shoulders, and her dress fluffed out like the softest, fluffiest cloud. She looked so confident and happy. I could not understand why my mother didn't want this for me.

"Mom, please—" I started.

"Paige," she said, looking up at the ceiling. "There are things you don't know, okay? I just don't want you to get hurt."

"I won't get hurt," I said. "I'll win." I was certain of that, too.

She paused. "I'll think about it."

I can't imagine how she thought about anything, though, with the amount of pestering I did.

"Can I do the pageant?" I asked her every hour for the rest of that night.

"Can I do it?" I asked at breakfast.

"You'll let me do the pageant, right?" I asked on the ride to school.

"I've seen pageants on television," I said when my mom picked me up at the end of the day. "Lots of girls earn money that they can use for college."

I heard my mother talk about money sometimes. She always said that her job—bartender at the American Legion—didn't pay nearly enough. "Do *we* have money to send me to college?"

She answered quietly. "No, Paige, we don't. Not yet."

Before bed, I said, "Oprah Winfrey did pageants, and look at her." I knew how much my mother loved Oprah.

She kissed me and said, "I'm thinking about it, Paige."

And she was. But she wasn't just thinking about yes or no. She was thinking that there were things in this world I did not yet know—things about myself. She was wondering what would happen if they found out about my HIV. Would they even allow an HIV-positive girl to enter pageants? What if we went, and they rejected me? It might hurt me more than if I'd never tried in the first place.

But at the same time, she was thinking something else: why *couldn't* an HIV-positive girl do pageants? I mean, there was nothing about my illness that would prevent me from being able to do the things that pageant contestants had to do. Really, what was so wrong with that idea?

When I asked the next morning, "Can I? Can I please?" she sighed.

"Okay." She closed her eyes and shook her head. I could tell she was wondering what she was getting us into.

By the time she opened them again, I was already rushing toward her. I threw my arms around her. "Oh, thank you, Mom! Thank you, thank you!"

"You're so young," she murmured, in a way that made it clear she wasn't really even talking to me. "The world is so complicated and you are so young."

"Don't worry, Mom," I said. My words were muffled against her body. "I'll win. I swear: they will love me."

She hugged me hard and whispered in my ear, "Yeah, they'll love you, Paige. I know it."

My mom was the mom who always said yes—even to Disneyland.
Here I am on my seventh birthday, celebrating with Donald and the gang.

Catching some sun in Myrtle Beach, South Carolina, with my mom.

Clarkstown

YASMINE

The girl I saw in the auditorium on that first day of sixth grade? I met her almost right away, in the lunchroom. Her name was Yasmine.

"What do you play?" I asked Yasmine as I opened up a bag of chips.

"I like soccer," she answered.

I laughed, tilted the open bag of chips in her direction. She took one.

"No, I mean I saw you carrying a musical instrument," I said. "Was it a violin?"

"Viola," she said. "Similar. I play piano, too. Do you play anything?"

"No, but I love to sing."

She nodded.

"And I like soccer, too."

She laughed. "Cool."

It happened just that easily, our beginning. Within a few days, we were sitting together every day at lunch, passing notes to each other in the hallway. Within a few weeks' time, she had become something else—a kind of friend I hadn't had before. She became my best friend.

Before long, I had learned every inch of the two-mile stretch between our two homes. Even now, all these years later, I could probably find my way to her house with my eyes closed. *Now we are passing the Little League fields on West 73rd, now we are turning right onto Ditch Road. On our right is Greenbriar Elementary School, where Yasmine went. On my left, the Abundant Harvest United Methodist and CrossBridge Baptist churches.* At the busy intersection with 86th Street, with its car washes and chain pharmacies and grocery stores and Office Depots, the trees started to seem more abundant, the houses a little larger.

In Yasmine's development, all the lawns had these little ADT security signs in them. Looking out the windows, I saw mothers power walking or pushing baby joggers. A block ahead, an older couple wearing visors walked hand in hand. It was a neighborhood of golden retrievers and potted plants on the front steps, of kids walking toward the clubhouse with tennis rackets slung casually over their shoulders.

Ordinarily, my mother wanted me to hang out with other kids back at our house: "If you're here, Paige," she always said, "I know you're safe." But Yasmine's father was stricter than my mom, and Yasmine's neighborhood was a safe one. My mom relented, on the condition that she could call me whenever she needed.

It was a slight burst of freedom, and it was deeply exciting to me.

At Yasmine's house, we spent hours and hours doing nothing at all. Sometimes, we sat on a big wooden swing in a park near her house. Other times, we'd play pool in what her family called the "great room," a large, airy space off her living room. We sprawled out on the floor and talked about sports and show choir, about how quickly boys and girls seemed to be pairing up. I liked the idea of boys. I loved the idea of having a boyfriend, but actual boys—the real boys I saw every day—still seemed so silly to me.

We looked at friends' online profiles, and we listened to our favorite song, Augustana's "Boston," over and over again, screeching the lyrics—*"She said I think I'll go to Boston, I think I'll start a new life, I think I'll start it over, where no one knows my name . . ."*—at the top of our lungs.

Sometimes, too, Yasmine and I hung out with her older sister, Lila, and her sister's best friend, Madison. They were both in eighth grade, and they shared their wisdom about sixth grade—which teachers were strict, which ones would notice if we copied each other's notes, which ones got really mad if you turned in homework late.

I loved being there. It was my home away from home.

One day when the leaves had changed color, my mom dropped me off at Yasmine's house. Yasmine must have been waiting at the window for me, because she came bursting out of the house as soon as we were in the driveway. Her cheeks were flushed. "Paige!" she exclaimed, running toward the car. "Guess what, Paige?"

Later, I would hear rumors that Yasmine was descended from exiled Middle Eastern royalty. When I heard that, I would think of this moment—of her pushing her way out the front door, and running toward my car in her bare feet. Yasmine seemed as grounded, as unpretentious, as anyone I have ever known.

My mother rolled down her window. "Hi, Yasmine," she said.

"Oh, hi, Mrs. Rawl," Yasmine said with a wave. She was jumping up and down, tiny little jumps. Whatever it was, whatever the excitement, she could not contain it.

I stepped out of the car. "What's up?" I asked Yasmine. "What is it?"

"Paige," my mom interrupted. "What are you going to do?"

"I'm going to call you at exactly five p.m.," I said the way I repeated it every time she dropped me off. I met Yasmine's eye and we both smiled ever so slightly. Yasmine knew how worried my mom always got.

"Right," said my mom. "Just check in to let me know you're safe. Now come give me a kiss."

"*Good-bye*, Mom . . ."

As my mom backed out of the driveway, I turned to Yasmine. "Okay, now what's so exciting?"

She closed her hands into fists and shook them excitedly above her head. "My dad's going to let Lila and me have a party at the clubhouse this summer. A really fancy one. For our birthdays."

I had never been inside Yasmine's neighborhood clubhouse, but whenever I drove past it, I could see a giant chandelier hanging by the two-story window. The clubhouse had a balcony that overlooked a pool, potted flowers, and a brick-and-iron fence wrapping all around the premises.

"No way!" I screamed.

"Yes, way!" We jumped up and down, right there in the driveway.

"Oh, my God, I seriously cannot wait," I said.

Inside, we lay down on the great-room floor and spent the afternoon dreaming about her party. Never mind that it was half a year away; it was all we could think about. There would be music and swimming, a dinner buffet and a dessert bar. There would be boys and girls, together, and we would sit at tables beneath blue-and-white umbrellas, surrounded by trees and planted gardens. We would make a toast with soda pop to everything good: to Yasmine and Lila, to friends, to summer, to growing up.

Yasmine and I talked about color schemes for the party, considered the merits of balloons and streamers, discussed the guest list until the light grew dark.

Then my phone rang. It was my mother. I had forgotten to call.

"Mom, I'm so sorry," I answered. "I totally forgot."

"I was worried," my mom said sharply. Then, with relief in her voice: "I just wanted to know you are okay."

"Mom, what was going to happen to me? I'm just at Yasmine's house."

"I know." She sighed. "I know. I just worry."

I rolled my eyes at Yasmine.

Yasmine leaned over and called into the phone. "Lila and I are going to have a birthday party at the clubhouse, Mrs. Rawl," she said.

"That sounds like fun," my mom shouted back.

"Okay, Mom. Now you know I'm safe, so I'm hanging up."

I turned back to Yasmine. "Your party is going to be like something straight out of TV."

"I know. I can't wait."

"I wish it were happening tomorrow." I sighed.

Dad

Perhaps you're wondering about my father. I can't really blame you; I wondered about him, too. I wondered about him for a long, long time.

But all I have to share is a single memory. It is literally the only memory I have of him, and it is not the happy sort of father-daughter memory that other girls get.

In March of 2001, I was six years old, near the end of my kindergarten year. Three years had passed since my mom and I had been diagnosed. We hadn't seen my father since, and I no longer had any memory of him. He was a complete stranger to me.

We were in the living room watching TV when we got the call. My dad's parents told my mom that my dad was in a hospital in Georgia. He had an AIDS-related infection, they said, and he wasn't expected to live much longer. If my mother wanted me to see my father, ever again, she'd have to bring me immediately.

I was just a little girl, so all I knew was that we got in the car first thing the next morning and drove until nightfall.

I have a photograph from that visit. My mom had taken it knowing that it would be the last photograph of us together. In the picture, I am sitting on the edge of my father's hospital bed. My usual grin is gone; I stare out at the camera, deadly serious. My father lies behind me. His mouth is open, his eyes are closed. Beside us is a stuffed angel I brought as a gift for him. In the center of the angel doll is a heart with a clear plastic sleeve; inside that sleeve my mom and I had slid a photograph of me, grinning out toward the camera. It is such a contrast: unsmiling me next to a smiling image of myself. It looks like I'm seated with a memory of a happier life.

While we sat in his room, my dad tried to speak to me, to my mother. His mouth opened and closed, but only a gurgling sound came out. Tears came out of his eyes, rolled down his cheek, and fell into dark spots on the hospital bed. After a while, he stopped. His mouth fell open again, and I knew he had fallen asleep.

When I woke in the hotel room, the morning after that visit, my mother told me that my father had died during the night.

I would never learn what he had been trying to say to us.

I would never, truth be told, understand my father at all.

My dad and me at my first birthday party.

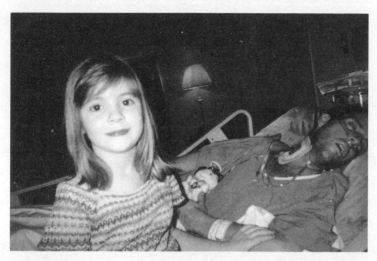

March 2001, the last time I saw my father. I was so young. Too young to understand much of what was happening, or why my father was so sick.

Clarkstown

LAUGHTER

One morning in sixth grade, just before lunch, a boy in my class misbehaved by talking back to a teacher. Miss Fischer punished the entire class by making us eat lunch in silence. We were not permitted to speak through the entire lunch period. We were silent as we slipped sandwiches out of paper bags, silent as we opened little cardboard cartons of milk. Then, when lunch was over, we stood silently to return to the classroom.

That's when a girl in front of me turned around. She made a face at me—her cheeks puffed out, her eyes widened. She looked like a balloon that had been overfilled, one that might burst any second and go flying all over the hallway. It lasted only a second or two, but that was enough. I burst out laughing. Quickly, I clamped my hand over my mouth, but I was shaking with laughter. I could not stop.

The monitor sent me to Miss Fischer's office, and suddenly everything seemed a lot less funny.

But there were a number of other sixth graders in Miss Fischer's office. Apparently, more than a few of us had trouble getting through lunch without giggling.

Miss Fischer folded her arms across her chest and looked at us sternly. We looked down, shifted awkwardly on our feet.

"I will ask you to write me an essay about why you shouldn't be suspended," she said to the group. "If you don't have it to me by tomorrow, you *will* be suspended."

My cheeks flushed. I stared down at my sneakers. I was supposed to go to Yasmine's house that night; I had finished my homework early so that I could go. Writing this essay would make that impossible.

When I told Yasmine I couldn't go to her house, that I had to stay home to write the essay, her eyes widened.

"Seriously? You really have to?"

"I do."

"For laughing?"

"Yeah," I said. I felt grateful that she looked as shocked as she did. I hated getting in trouble, and somehow Yasmine's reaction made me feel better about the whole thing—like maybe I wasn't that bad, maybe the whole thing really was just a little crazy.

"What are you going to write?"

I shrugged. "I don't know," I said. "But I *want* to say that laughing doesn't really seem like something a kid should be suspended for."

Yasmine grinned. "As the very proud principal of Clarkstown Middle School," she said, her impression dead-on, "I declare that happiness is an offense punishable by suspension."

Now I was grinning. Yasmine always made me feel better about things.

"I am the very proud principal of children who never, ever laugh," she continued. "You laugh, we punish. At Clarkstown, we prefer our children to be unhappy."

And just like that, I felt better. I had been upset since lunch for having gotten myself in trouble. Suddenly, it didn't seem so important anymore.

That was the thing about having a best friend; simply sharing a bad situation with her was enough to make it go away.

. . .

I'd like to explain why, precisely, Yasmine and I became so close. Maybe if I could boil it down to a simple formula—my friendliness + her intensity; or my optimism + her sensibility— then it wouldn't have been such a big a deal when it all turned sour.

But it wasn't that way, of course. Who can explain what makes two people connect? All I know is that at the start of sixth grade, as lockers clanged and kids stuffed cell phones into their pockets before dashing off to science class, I had a friend the likes of which I hadn't known before. I barely needed anyone else.

I trusted her, wholly.

First Pageant

These days, what most people know about pageants comes straight from reality TV.

They're funny, these television shows. They feature pushy stage moms who force their toddlers to prance onstage while wearing stuffed bras and fake, rounded rumps. These moms are outrageous: they encourage their young children to smoke fake cigarettes onstage, they dress their toddlers in skimpy costumes, and pit one twin against another in an effort to win.

All of these families are picked for ratings, of course. I know, because I've done pageants for over a decade, and I will tell you I've never once seen a child dressed like Julia Roberts's character in *Pretty Woman*.

For me, pageants have always been a combination of four of the things I love most in the world: dressing up, singing onstage, speaking in front of people, and meeting new friends. They've helped me think on the spot and respond to all kinds of situations with warmth. They've taught me grace under pressure, how to encourage others, and what it means to think about community.

I loved them from the very start.

My mom signed me up for the Sweetheart pageant, the one from the brochure. I loved every second of it. I loved my floor-length lace-and-satin dress. The new haircut my mom had given me for the occasion (she'd snipped me some brand-new bangs in the bathroom just the night before, and I swear: she did a great job).

Most of all, I loved being backstage with all those other girls.

The first friend I made was Annie Edge. She was my age exactly and although that made her a competitor in our division, it sure didn't *feel* like we were in competition. Annie had done plenty of pageants before, and she took it upon herself to become my personal tour guide to this amazing new world. For example, as we stood in line waiting for our one-on-one judges' interviews, I noticed that the judges were handing some girls bananas.

"Why do they have to hold a piece of fruit?" I whispered.

"You are supposed to pretend it's a phone," she whispered back. "Sometimes they want to see you have a conversation."

"With who?"

"Whoever you choose. Just make sure you sound friendly and grown-up."

I liked that—using my imagination and acting grown up all in the same moment. I decided if they gave me a banana I would talk to Dr. Cox and pretend she was hiring me to work as a pediatric doctor. "Yes," I would say. "Yes, I absolutely adore children."

"Annie Edge?" one of the judges called.

She turned to me and raised her eyebrows in excitement. "Wish me luck, Paige."

"Good luck," I whispered. And I meant it.

"You too." She grinned, and I could tell she meant it, too.

I didn't get the banana question. Instead, the judge asked me if I would rather be a train engine or a caboose.

"Engine," I said confidently.

The judge asked why, and I responded, "Because I would

rather be a leader than a follower."

I was proud of myself, then. Really proud, because it is hard to be asked a random question and come up with an answer—a good answer—on the spot like that.

I couldn't wait to tell Annie how I had done.

Later, I made another friend, too.

We'd been rehearsing for the sportswear competition, and I thought I knew what I was supposed to do: I was supposed to show off my outfit—white skirt, white blouse, both embroidered with pretty blue flowers. Music played over the speakers, and someone was reading a description of my outfit into a microphone. I stood there, smiling, one hand on my hip. I stood the way I thought people would want me to.

That's when one of the bigger girls, from an older division, leapt onstage. She was tall—taller even than my mother—and crazy beautiful, with long blond hair and very full lips and piercing blue eyes.

"You need a routine," she said. When I stared back at her, not understanding, she smiled. "Here, let me show you." She told me her name was Heather. Then showed me how to step in time to the music, look over my shoulder, and then pause, giving the audience a chance to really see my outfit.

"Look confident," Heather said. "It's all about confidence. Have fun with it. Be yourself."

So I did. I listened to the music, and I *step, step, stepped.* I spun. I looked over my shoulder the way she did. Then I did it the way that felt right to me.

The music pulsed. *Step, step, step.* I put my hand on my hip. I waved at the audience.

Heather smiled, her crystal eyes twinkling. "That's great! You've got such good energy. I'll bet you do really well."

Then this girl—this girl gorgeous enough to be a model, or Miss Indiana herself—hugged me.

God, it was just so much fun to be there.

The pageant flew by, a whirlwind of laughter, outfit changes, and *how do I look*s. Kids belted songs into microphone, danced in sync, and waved with all their hearts. I did it, too, and I'm telling you: every moment I was there, I felt myself becoming more confident, as if I were growing taller simply from being there.

I felt like I was reaching toward something, becoming a newer, friendlier version of myself.

If I could have stopped time, I would have. But one event led to another, and before I knew it, it was almost over.

Just before they announced the winners in our division, Annie whispered to me, "Guess what's in my shoe." We were standing backstage in our sparkling gowns, about to take our place for the big finale.

"What's in your shoe?" I asked. I remember thinking, *What a funny thing to say. What in the world could be in her shoe right now?*

The girls were starting to walk out on stage, one at a time.

This was it: our big finish. We were about to find out who won.

Quickly Annie slipped off her shoe. She reached in and lifted out a piece of paper. It said, in handwriting that I could tell was her own: *The winner of the Sweetheart Division 2003 is . . . Annie Edge.*

I grinned at her. It seemed like such a good idea—hoping for something so much that you write it down and keep it with you everywhere. Like a way of making it happen just by thinking hard enough. I wished I'd thought of it.

"*Hurry*," said one of the organizers. "It's time." Annie shoved the note back in her shoe, and slipped the whole thing back on her foot. In an instant, she and I were back onstage, smiling and waving with all our hearts.

The music played loudly, and lots of people in the audience held up cameras. I searched the room for my mom, and there she was, near the front. She was seated next to Heather's mom, and she was beaming at me. She really did look like she was having a great time.

I suspected that she, too, was happy that she'd agreed to let me do this.

As the judges started to call the names of the winners, my mom and Heather's mom leaned into each other, just a little bit, for support. My mom clasped her hands together and pressed them against her forehead. Heather's mom rubbed her hands against her thigh. Both of them closed their eyes. It looked a little bit like they were praying.

I liked that she'd made a friend, too. I liked that this stranger, Heather's mom, was rooting for me, almost as much as my mom was.

The judges announced the fourth runner-up. It wasn't me, and it wasn't Annie. I caught Annie's eye and we both smiled, ever so slightly. Annie looked so confident.

They announced the third runner-up. Again, it wasn't either one of us. I saw my mom take a huge breath.

And then they announced the second runner-up. It was me.

I gasped. Out in the audience, my mother's eyes popped open. She applauded hard and beamed at me, her face a mixture of pride and wonder.

Someone handed me a trophy. They handed me flowers—a bouquet of big, white roses. I took them and beamed.

My heart pounded. My cheeks ached from smiling. I was

so thrilled, I barely even noticed the first runner-up. But then, when they called the winner, the winner of our whole division—it was Annie!

Everyone cheered, but I swear, I might have been cheering loudest of all.

All smiles after being crowned second runner-up at the Miss Indiana Sweetheart pageant.

. . .

We said our good-byes in a flurry. I hugged Annie, I hugged Heather, I hugged a bunch of other girls. My mom, I think, hugged everyone in the room. She and Heather's mom exchanged numbers, and I was so glad, because it meant I would see Heather again.

"Just remember what I said, Paige," Heather said. "Be yourself."

I waved good-bye, then Mom wrapped an arm around my shoulder and walked with me to the car.

On the way home, with my trophy and flowers in my lap, I thought about that note Annie had written: *The winner of the Sweetheart pageant 2003 is . . . Annie Edge.*

It is a good idea, I thought. *It is a very good idea to write a note like that and slip it in your shoe.* I decided right then that I was going to do the same thing next year.

And there would be a next year, I promised myself. I was determined.

There was a next year. Then many more pageants after that.

When I returned to the Sweetheart pageant I slipped a note in my own shoe: *The winner of the Sweetheart pageant 2004 is . . . Paige Rawl.*

And it worked. I won.

Annie, the reigning Sweetheart, placed the crown on my head. We met each other's eyes and Annie beamed. My whole body felt so light—like I could walk on air. I knew I had never, ever been that happy.

That win confirmed something for me. It taught me that if you just believed something hard enough, you could make anything come true.

Of course, a day would come when I would learn that it's not enough to want something, even to want it with all your heart. But in those early pageant days, when the world seemed to be opening up all around me, all I understood was that confidence was everything. And I had that in spades.

I could make anything happen. *Anything at all.*

*I loved everything about being in pageants. Here I am
serving as the Miss Indiana Sweetheart State Hostess.*

Clarkstown

XLI

In February, the Colts played their first Super Bowl since 1971.

For weeks prior to Super Bowl XLI, the city was plastered in Colts blue. The upturned horseshoe that is the team's logo appeared everywhere—in yard signs, in store windows, on jackets and hats and backpacks. Even babies wore pajamas emblazoned with the logo.

On Sunday, February 4, Yasmine and I watched together as the Colts defeated the Chicago Bears 29 to 17 in the pouring rain. The team's quarterback, Peyton Manning, completed twenty-five of thirty-eight passes, even as players slipped and slid all over the muddy field.

It was the Colts' first win since they left Baltimore to become our hometown team, and it was the first major professional sports victory for Indianapolis in nearly thirty years.

When the game ended, we could hear house upon house, the entire city it seemed, explode in cheers.

I texted my mom almost immediately: *They won!!!!!!*

I knew she would know, of course. But she would want to hear from me.

She texted back: *I know!!!! Best team ever!!!*

I spent the night at Yasmine's house; Madison slept over with Lila, too. We were so excited we barely slept.

In the morning, on the bus to school, all the kids wore Colts blue. A group of kids were talking about the victory parade—the Colts were scheduled to arrive in a ticker-tape parade that day. Madison said wistfully, "I wish we could go."

"Yeah, me too," I said. Last night was so exciting. The whole city was so happy, and now we were just going to shuffle between boring classes at Clarkstown Middle School.

That's when I got an idea. I looked up excitedly, glanced from Yasmine to Madison to Lila, then back to Yasmine.

"Let's call my mom," I said.

Lila rolled her eyes. "She'll never say yes."

"I don't know," I said slowly. "My mom might, actually."

And the more I thought about it, the more it seemed like she really might. My mom, after all, was still the mom who said yes.

Yes, we can turn the song up loud.

Yes, I will take you and your friends to the water park.

Yes, whatever it is, as long as you take your medicine and call me and don't make me worry any more than I already do—as long as I can be with you and know you are safe—yes, yes, yes.

When Mom answered her phone, I told her about the parade. "Can we go?" I pleaded.

Yasmine leaned over my shoulder and shouted in the direction of the phone, "Yes, please, can we, Mrs. Rawl?!"

Then Madison and Lila joined in: "Please take us, Mrs. Rawl! Please!"

I held up the phone so she could hear them plead.

When I put the phone back to my ear, my mother was speaking. ". . . their parents will have to say okay."

I covered the phone with my hands and looked up at my friends. "Oh, my God, I think she's saying yes," I whispered. Their eyes widened in disbelief. "But only if everybody's parents say okay."

The next half hour was a flurry of phone calls, of reassurances and promises that somehow—magically—worked. We had "Colts Fever" to thank; it had apparently captured us all. We walked into school just long enough to put our belongings in our lockers. A few minutes later, we sat outside the main office, watching kids come into school for the day.

That's when I saw a girl I knew. Amber was in seventh grade, a cheerleader. She had crazy curly hair, which she always just pulled back in a rough ponytail like she didn't give a hoot. She walked with her mother, who looked young—about a decade younger than my own mom—and very pretty.

Something was wrong, though. They walked slowly, and it almost looked like Amber was holding her mother up. Her mom's arm rested on Amber's shoulder. She took tiny steps, as if she were afraid she'd trip.

Amber's mom stumbled a little, and Amber wrapped her arm tight around her mom's waist to catch her.

We must have been staring, because Amber's eyes flashed toward us, fiercely. "Can I help you?" she asked, her eyes narrowed.

I looked away quickly. Amber snapped, "Can one of you at least make yourself useful? Hold the door for us, maybe?"

I jumped up and held the door to the office open for them.

Amber's mom smiled at me as she walked through the door, and Amber, still bracing her mom, said quietly, "Thanks, Paige."

Moments later, my mother rolled up in front of the school. We signed out, stepped out into the winter air, and climbed into her car. We giggled excitedly. We forgot all about Amber, all about Clarkstown and classes and textbooks.

The day was bitter cold, in the single digits, with the radio newscaster announcing that the wind chill made it feel like it was below zero.

We parked downtown, joined the crowds lining up on the sidewalk, and we waited.

The streets were a sea of blue and white. Around us, people held signs: WE LOVE YOU, COLTS, or simply, THANK YOU, COLTS. There were camera crews everywhere. Cars honked their horns as they passed. Each time they honked, the crowd cheered in response, holding up forefingers in a show of "We're number one!"

My toes and fingers were numb, but it didn't matter. This was a whirlwind party—"a once-in-a-lifetime party," everyone kept saying.

We waited. Afternoon came. A heavyset man walked up and down on the street, calling out to the crowd, "We've waited all day? Hell no, we've waited years. Let's get loud!!!" Fans hollered and whooped and cheered in response.

Day gave way to darker skies, and lights went on inside the office buildings around us. And then, right when the day was at the edge of darkness, it happened.

I knew that the team had arrived before I could see them. It was unmistakable: the crowd, which had been cheering off and on all day, suddenly reached a fever pitch. Almost instantly, all around us, arms were raised in a show of victory.

I turned to Yasmine. "They're here," I said. "They're really here!"

We craned our necks to see past all the Colts fans. Yasmine was taller, and she saw them first.

"Here they are!" she cried. I jumped up and down trying to catch a glimpse.

And then I saw them. They *were* there, right there: the Colts—our team, our home team. Some players rolled along on floats, others waved from the backs of pickup trucks.

At first, I saw only the vehicles, but then I saw the players themselves, their arms spread wide, embracing the crowd's roars with obvious pride and glee.

They were real, and they were really there.

People screamed, shook their signs and flags, called out messages of love that were impossible to hear over all the shouting. It was incredible to me, the way, in this single instant, an entire city's energy was directed right at one place.

It was electric, absolutely thrilling.

And then Yasmine gripped my arm, and I saw him. Peyton Manning. Right there, right in front of us. He stood inside a moving car, his head poking out of a sunroof. He waved and grinned at the crowd. After all these months seeing him on television, there he was in the flesh. It was actually *him*. I screamed at the top of my lungs and waved my arm wildly at him.

"MVP!" people chanted. "MVP!"

I begin chanting it, too.

When he passed, Yasmine and I looked at each other and hugged.

Everything was amazing. Endless victories lay ahead.

Understanding

No one stays a child forever. Just as my sippy cups gave way to glassware and my powdered medicine gave way to pills, as I grew older, I began to pay more attention in those doctor's visits. I didn't ask many questions, but I noticed I heard certain words repeated: HIV. Immune system. T-cells. Viral load. I didn't know what they meant, exactly, but I had begun to notice how serious my mother's face was in those visits, the look of relief that came over her as Dr. Cox read numbers out of my chart.

In fourth grade, I visited the dentist for a checkup. My chart lay open on the table next to me, and I glanced down. At the bottom of the chart were two handwritten words, both circled in black pen: *Asthma* was one. *HIV+* was the other.

Later, when I was in fifth grade, I heard the words "HIV/ AIDS" in a health class. I pictured Dr. Cox's waiting room, filled with pamphlets like *HIV/AIDS: Get the Facts.* I remembered my father lying in his hospital bed, the tears in his eyes as he opened his mouth, then closed it again.

I began to wonder.

One spring day, five years after my father died—just a short time before I met Yasmine—my mom picked me up from school. I didn't say a word for most of the drive. Then, when we pulled into the driveway of our house, Radio Disney pulsing through our speakers, I asked my mother a simple question: "Am I HIV positive or negative?"

My mother took a deep breath, then parked the car. She

took me into the kitchen, sat me in the tall stool at the kitchen counter, the one where she'd served me countless meals. She stood on the other side of the counter, leaned in toward me, and told me the truth: that I'd been HIV positive since birth.

That HIV was a blood disease.

That she'd wanted to tell me for a long time, but hadn't known how.

That she knew it would raise complicated questions for me, including some about my father's death.

That she hadn't wanted to scare me.

That we would talk lots more about it as I got older.

That she had it, too.

That we would be okay. That as long as we both took our medicine and took care of ourselves everything would be okay.

Then she made me my favorite meal, spaghetti with meatballs. After we ate, we did what we often enjoyed in the evenings: we belted out oldies tunes together into our karaoke machine. We sang and sang, our bare feet dancing on the carpet of our living-room floor. My mom tucked me into bed that night, just like she always did. She kissed my forehead before turning out the light.

I rolled onto my side and listened to the sound of my own breath.

Everything was the same, and everything was different, all at once.

Lock-in

One month after the Super Bowl parade, Clarkstown Middle School held a "lock-in"—a dusk-to-dawn, chaperoned slumber party at the school. The school was filled with different stations—a dancing station, a station where you could play board games, a snack station, a sports station.

Yasmine and I dashed from one station to another. We ate junk food from the concession stand, guzzled soda directly from the cans. We danced to Justin Timberlake and Rihanna. We dashed to the board game station, watched for a few minutes, then ran back for more snacks. It was so strange. We were at school, but for once our only job was to play and talk and laugh.

Then we wandered into the gym. A group of seventh graders, mostly boys, were shooting hoops. There was just one girl among them—Amber, the girl I'd seen holding up her mother outside the building on the day of the Colts parade.

Lila and Madison sat on the floor with some other girls. Yasmine walked over toward them, while I watched the basketball players.

"Hey, Paige." Amber waved.

I walked over.

"Hey, is it true you do pageants?" she asked.

"Yeah."

"You wear ball gowns and stuff?"

"Evening wear. Yeah."

"Swimsuits?"

I laughed. "No. In fact, we wear church-like outfits for the interview portion. Dresses or business suits."

"Ugh. I hate dresses."

She picked up a basketball and started dribbling it, moving away from the boys, toward one of the other baskets.

"Come play," she said. I followed her.

"You do that on weekends?" she asked.

"Summers mostly," I said.

"You ever win?"

"I have," I said. "I did once, anyway. I've also been a runner-up."

I wasn't sure if she would make fun of me then—she didn't seem like the kind of girl that would get excited about pageants. But instead she stuck out her lower lip, like she was impressed.

"Cool," she said.

Amber and I took turns casually shooting baskets. On the other side of the gym, the boys she'd been playing with were playing a more intense game. Some of the best players on the boys' basketball team were there—Kyle Walker and Michael Jepson and Devin Holt, all seventh graders—along with a handful of others.

One of them was a boy with dark, shaggy hair. He was wiry, with a long, thin face. He wasn't exactly handsome, but he smiled a lot. I liked his eyes. There was something kind about those eyes. I watched him for a while, and he must have sensed it. He looked up, right at me.

I immediately looked away.

Amber dribbled for a while. "Holy crap, it's just so nice to be out of my house," she said. "My family had to move last week, and our whole life is in boxes back home."

She took a shot at the basket, jumping a little as she threw. The ball bounced off the metal rim.

"Why'd you have to move?" I asked.

She grabbed the rebound, then bounce-passed the ball to me. "My mom has MS."

I caught the ball and dribbled it a few times. "MS?" I asked. I tossed the ball toward the basket. It hit the backboard, nowhere near the basket. It bounced back toward us, and Amber grabbed it.

"Multiple sclerosis," she said. She dribbled the ball a couple of times, then stopped. "It's where your immune system attacks your central nervous system. Isn't that a bitch?"

I didn't know what to say, so I looked out at the boys' game. The boy with shaggy hair dribbled the ball past Kyle.

"Makes it really hard for her to walk sometimes," said Amber. "We needed a smaller place because it's so hard for her to get around."

That's when she noticed me watching the boys.

"Hey, who are you looking at, anyway?" She followed my gaze. "Ethan?"

I felt my cheeks flush red.

"Huh. Ethan's a really great guy," she said. "But kinda goofy."

And then, as if on command, he looked up at us. When he saw we were watching, he made a big show of running across the floor with huge, slow strides like he was in slow motion. Then he purposefully and dramatically tripped over his own feet, tossing the basketball out in front of him. A moment later, he lay on his belly, his legs splayed behind him.

Amber burst out laughing. "He's always doing stupid stuff like that."

Just then, Devin Holt picked up the ball that Ethan had let bounce away, and he threw it at us.

"What the fuck?" Amber shouted, hurling it back at him.

She turned back to me. "Sorry," she said. She shrugged. "The F-word is my favorite word."

"You know, you don't exactly seem like a cheerleader," I said.

She shrugged. "I like being loud," she said. "And I hate sitting down. I'll take any sport that lets me jump and shout. Why, you want to cheer next year?"

I nodded.

"Want me to show you a couple of cheers?"

"Yes!" I exclaimed. And right as I did, I looked at Ethan, and at that exact moment he looked at me. Our eyes met, and my cheeks flushed red.

"Oh, my God," said Amber, shaking her head. "I can't believe you like *Ethan*."

Somewhere in the early hours of the morning, a few hours after I shot baskets with Amber, Yasmine and I were seated on top of a table outside the gym. I peeled back a wrapper on a Kit Kat bar and crossed my legs. We talked.

Nearby, in the girls' bathroom, I knew a bunch of girls were looking in the mirror, reapplying thick mascara, smacking their glossy lips at their own images. I felt good that we were out here. Neither Yasmine nor I wore much makeup, and it was a relief to have a friend who was so down-to-earth.

That's when Yasmine said, "I'm a little worried." She shook out some candies from a box of Nerds and popped them in her mouth.

"What about?" I asked. I thought she was saying something about tonight, some mild worry about the lock-in. Like, what if she got really tired and wanted to go home?

Instead, she told me something I didn't know. She told me about a family member who had not been well. The family member was going to live with her. She was worried, about this person, worried about some erratic behavior, worried about the effect the illness would have on her whole family.

I understood that she was telling me something important. I wanted her to feel better, to feel less alone.

"Everybody's got something," I told her. I thought about Amber's mom, needing a small apartment because of her MS, so she wouldn't have to take too many steps. I thought about all those kids I saw at Riley all the time—the ones in wheelchairs or with crutches or bald heads.

And then I told her that I had something, too.

I told her I had HIV.

If her face changed at all when I told her, I didn't notice it. If she looked at me differently, I didn't see it. But of course, I would not have been looking for it. I mean, I knew kids who had diabetes, kids who had knee troubles, kids who had acne. I really meant what I said to Yasmine: everybody had something. HIV just happened to be my thing.

A group of kids walked over and we began talking to them. Then Amber poked her head out of the gym. "Hey, Paige," she said. "We need one more kid to help us practice our L-up." An L-up was one of the basic cheerleading stunts—one where someone gets lifted in the air. It looks effortless, even though I knew it took a ton of practice.

"Sure!" I said, scrambling down.

We practiced several times, the seventh-grade girls lifting me high into the air until I was standing near their shoulders, my arms extended toward the ceiling.

I was happy then. I remember that.

A little while later, Yasmine and I were back outside the gym, sitting at the tables with a big group of kids. I was sweaty from all that activity. Nothing looked any different than it had an hour ago. One of the kids passed around a water bottle. I took a swig, then handed it back.

"Careful," a seventh-grade boy said. "Don't drink after her. She has AIDS."

It took me a moment to register what I had just heard. Then it took me another moment to make sense of it.

Forget the fact that I had HIV, not AIDS—I knew exactly who he was talking about. He was talking about me.

I didn't look at Yasmine directly, although she was right there. She surely heard it, too.

She has AIDS.

But.

But wait.

There was only one way anyone could possibly know I had HIV.

Don't drink after her.

I told only one person. Just one.

I told my best friend.

My body went slightly cold, and I felt a wave of nausea.

If I told only Yasmine, and now other people knew, this meant only one thing: Yasmine had told someone else. She must have done it immediately, probably while I was practicing the Wildcats cheer.

But she couldn't have. She *wouldn't* have.

Lila, I thought. She might have told Lila.

Don't drink after her.

Then Lila must have told other people. And those people were going to tell other people.

It was only an hour later and already everyone around me knew.

She has AIDS.

And I knew something else, just by the way he said it. I knew that my HIV wasn't the same as my asthma or somebody else's knee troubles. It was clear from how he said it that there was something really wrong with having HIV.

There was something wrong with *me*.

Everyone was looking at me. My cheeks felt hot, though I didn't know if it was from shame or anger.

The water bottle was still in my hand. I didn't dare pass it to anyone.

Just then, a song we all liked came on in the gym. The group jumped up and rushed toward the music to dance. I was just sitting there, still holding the water bottle from which no one else wanted to drink.

I didn't say anything to anyone about what just happened. I didn't say anything when I followed them into the gym to dance, and I didn't say anything to anybody when we headed back to the concession stand for popcorn. I didn't say anything when we listened to song after song, or even in the wee hours of the morning when everybody got sleepy and silly.

I didn't feel sleepy and silly.

I didn't say anything to Yasmine for the rest of the night, but I didn't act angry, either. Instead, I pretended it hadn't happened, that I hadn't heard what I heard, that people didn't know what they shouldn't know. I laughed a little too loudly and I danced with a little too much enthusiasm, occasionally sneaking glimpses of Ethan and wondering what he would think if he found out.

Mostly, I just tried to fit in.

But for the rest of the night, I was deeply conscious of Yasmine, of where she was at every moment. I was waiting, perhaps, for some kind of explanation.

She has AIDS.

Morning came with no explanation. The lock-in ended. My mom's car was waiting outside in the parking lot. I climbed into the front seat and looked back at the school.

"Did you love it?" Mom asked as she turned onto 73rd Street. She was so certain that the lock-in would have been fun—in her mind, there was simply no other possibility. I placed my head against the passenger window and looked outside. I didn't want to disappoint her.

"Yeah, it was good," I said. I heard my own voice, heard the sadness in it. "I'm tired," I added quickly. I turned on the radio.

At home, I took my medicine, my mother watching closely, then I lay down on my bed. I looked at my bright purple walls, the pink-and-purple spattered ceiling fan. On the other side of the wall, I heard my mother taking her pills—the opening of the cabinet door, the pills rattling around inside the plastic jar, the water running, then everything being put away all over again.

I placed a pillow over my head. I didn't want to think about the fact that she took medicine, too. I didn't want to think about her at all.

I felt sick to my stomach.

I didn't tell my mom about what had happened at the lock-in. Not then, not for the rest of the weekend, not for a long time.

Ordinarily, Yasmine would have called me. Mere hours would have passed before my phone would ring; Yasmine would be at the other end, ready to talk about all the gossip from the lock-in. We would have talked and talked, processing the event as we discussed it. Then we would have begged our parents to let us get together, so we could gossip about the lock-in face-to-face, even though we had just done exactly that on the phone.

But my phone didn't ring. Yasmine didn't call. She didn't call that day or that evening or even the next day. Which, frankly, was okay. I had no idea what I'd say to her, anyway.

Deny It

That spring, about a month after the lock-in, something happened. It was something about a note, something I don't understand exactly, even today, years after it happened. I have reconstructed the day in my mind many times, trying to figure out who was behind it, and why.

All I know, even today, is that this day marked the end of one part of my Clarkstown experience and the start of something else.

It was just after lunch. Yasmine and I had sat at opposite ends of the lunch table. We had not met each other's eye. We laughed and chatted with those who sat between us, each of us acting like there was nobody whatsoever—nobody at all, let alone a former best friend—in the space where the other sat a few feet away.

I had not spoken to Yasmine since the lock-in. Or perhaps it was she who hadn't spoken to me. Either way, she had retreated quickly into the distance, just as suddenly as she emerged as my friend at the start of the year.

I wondered if perhaps she felt bad about telling people about my HIV. I tried smiling at her in the hallway a couple of times, thinking maybe we could just start over. She didn't look at me to notice.

Anyway, on this day, I was walking toward social studies class when Yasmine rushed past me. She pressed her hand against her face, and her shoulders were rounded. I knew right away that she was crying. I stopped and glanced back at her as she raced down the hallway, her form moving swiftly around other kids, all those kids with textbooks under their arms, backpacks slung casually over one shoulder.

A few months ago, I wouldn't have hesitated to go after her, to weave through all those kids and stop her, help her, make her laugh again.

But now—I just knew she wouldn't even let me near her now.

She disappeared around a corner. I turned back toward class, but a group of girls blocked my way.

"God, Paige," one of them said, standing closer to me than was comfortable. "Why would you *do* that?"

"Yeah," followed another. "You're just mean."

I glanced from girl to girl. One set of eyes narrowed into angry slits, another bore into my own with a long, hard power stare.

But what was this about? Why would I do *what*?

The bell rang. I brushed past them, into class. My teacher stopped me at the door.

"Paige," he said quietly. "Miss Ward wants to see you in her office."

Miss Ward was one of the school counselors. My mom had been right on that first day—school counselors did seem to deal mostly with kids who were in trouble. Until now, Miss Ward was just the lady with all the makeup and the big flashy smile, the one who once had been my mother's gym teacher and now wore high heels and dealt with kids who had problems bigger than mine.

But I was in trouble now. I was sure of it. For the life of me, though, I had no idea why.

I glanced at my teacher, hoping he could give me some hint about what I'd done. He shrugged, then gestured toward the door. "Go ahead, Paige. We'll be right here when you get back."

Moments later, I knocked tentatively on Miss Ward's door. She looked up.

"Paige," she said sharply. "Please"—she gestured toward a chair on the other side of her desk—"sit."

I sat.

She folded her hands on her desk and said nothing for a long time. She just sat there looking at me. I shifted in my seat and stared down at my hands. Was I supposed to speak first? If so, what was I supposed to say?

There were framed diplomas on the wall above her. I glanced past her, toward the open window. I waited.

Finally, she spoke. "Paige, I'd like to know what you were thinking when you wrote that note."

"What?" I asked.

"The note that you put in Yasmine's locker," she said. "I want to know why you would write such a thing."

I tried to piece together what she was saying. I hadn't left a note in Yasmine's locker—not since before the lock-in, anyway. Could Yasmine have found a note that I left before the lock-in? But why would I be in trouble for that?

I looked at Miss Ward, confused. "What note?"

She frowned at me, looked me up and down for a moment.

Then she picked up a piece of paper. She held it out me.

Her nails were painted immaculately in bright red. I wondered, briefly, if they were press-ons.

When I didn't reach for the paper right away, she shook it a little.

I took it, unfolded it. I didn't recognize the handwriting.

Still. Some of the words jumped off the page immediately. *Terrorist* was one. *Go home* were others. I felt a cold rush go through my body. Oh, God, I didn't even want to look at this thing.

And then I saw. At the bottom of the page was my own name.

My name, as if I had written and signed this thing.

Wait, I thought. My brain seemed to be working slowly, more slowly than it should have. *Why would my name be on this?*

Then I realized that someone must have signed my name, pretending that I wrote this.

Someone signed my name to this? To a note that calls Yasmine a terrorist? But why . . . ?

I thrust it back toward Miss Ward, as if simply holding this thing was enough to get me in trouble. "That's not mine," I said quickly.

Her eyes were cool. The woman clearly didn't believe me.

"I didn't write that," I said again, as if merely repeating myself might change her mind.

I tried to fit together the pieces of this creepy puzzle. Honestly, though, none of this made any sense. It was my name, but it was not my handwriting. It was in Yasmine's locker, but I hadn't put it there.

Why would anyone . . . ?

That's when it hit me: someone out there hated me. Someone hated me so much that they wanted me to get in serious trouble. To this person, whoever it was, it was worth making Yasmine cry, worth disrupting the school day, worth throwing around words like *terrorist*—as hate-filled a word as could be imagined in Indiana in 2007.

I swallowed and touched my index and middle fingers to my temples. The world around me began closing in. It was like a camera lens focusing in on a smaller and smaller point. The fluorescent lights and the cinder-block walls, Miss Ward's frown and all my troubles with Yasmine, the fact that I was missing class right now for something I hadn't done: all of these things just disappeared as the world became centered on just a single thought. That thought, the only thing I could see then, was this: *People hate me.*

"You're saying you did NOT write this note?" Miss Ward's words, the sharpness with which she said them, jolted me.

I shook my head, although convincing her of my innocence suddenly seemed less important than it had been a few moments ago. It was the hate I was worried about now, the hate that seemed to be coming right out of that note, right at me.

I spoke quietly. "I didn't write it."

Miss Ward pressed her lips together and surveyed me for a moment. Then she stood up, walked to the door with a *click click click*, and called out to a staff member outside her office. "Could you please gather some samples of Paige's handwriting?" Her voice was curt.

She returned to her seat—*click click click*—then folded her arms across her chest. She took a deep breath. Then she frowned. "What on earth is going on here, Paige?"

And that's when I told her. I said that ever since the lock-in, Yasmine had been telling people that I had AIDS. I explained that it *had* to be Yasmine. No one else at school had known, and now everyone knew. I told her that kids were telling others not to drink after me, that they whispered about me in the hallway, that people had been treating me like I was contaminated.

I took some deep breaths, and I stared at her computer keyboard, not blinking. I was trying so hard to maintain my composure, but it did not work. My face crumpled, and I began crying. Hard.

"Half of them don't even know what HIV is, I'll bet." My face was twisted up. "They're just using it as an excuse to be mean." I was such a jumble of mad and sad, it was almost impossible to get my words out.

Then I wiped my eyes with the back of my hand. I looked at her, helpless.

"But," Miss Ward started, then she paused. She examined me curiously. "Well, but you don't have HIV . . . do you?"

"Well . . ." I paused. "Well, yeah. I do."

Miss Ward's face changed then. It froze for an instant, then drained of color. I swear, her skin grew so white that her makeup looked like a pastel mask.

She pressed her lips together and swallowed. "I see."

She began to stand up, then she sat down again. Her phone rang, but she did not pick it up—she just sat there with that blank look on her face. When the phone stopped ringing, she took a deep breath. Then her lipstick-red mouth widened into an enormous smile. Her blushed cheeks pulled toward her ears, and her giant earrings flashed.

"Well," she said brightly. "You know what you could do?"

She leaned in toward me like the two of us were about to share a delightful secret. "You could just deny having HIV!"

She beamed at me. The way she said it made it seem like that was the answer to everything.

I sat in silence for a long time, trying to make sense of her words, trying to figure out how her suggestion was helpful in any way.

Because, of course, I *did* have HIV. Saying I didn't would be a lie.

I had been raised my whole life to know that lying was wrong.

And there was something else, too. Something that was

very wrong with her words, with her suggestion. Something I couldn't quite put a finger on.

There was a knock at the door. The staff member that Miss Ward had assigned to gathering my work handed her several pieces of paper. I recognized them as some of my assignments—a composition, a vocabulary test, a piece of homework. Together, Miss Ward and the woman looked back and forth between the note to Yasmine and my own work. Miss Ward said quietly, "It wasn't her."

Okay, I thought. *This is it*. Now I would be able to leave her office, go back to class. After all, *I hadn't done it*, and now, in front of us, was proof.

Instead, Miss Ward pressed her lips into a frown. She stepped out of the room. When she returned a few minutes later, she was with three other people: another counselor, the assistant principal, and Yasmine.

The three of them filed in, sat down. Yasmine was sniffling, and she did not look at me.

I wanted to tell Yasmine, right then. I wanted to say that I didn't write the note, that they had compared handwriting and it was clear. I hadn't done it. I wanted to say to her: *Don't you know my handwriting? Don't you know me?* For some reason, I even wanted to say that I was sorry. I was sorry that she had gotten the note, sorry that there was this terrible gulf between us.

I was sorry, so completely sorry, that everything in the world was so confusing.

But I said nothing. I just sat there in silence waiting for one of the adults to take the lead.

But Miss Ward did not tell Yasmine that the note wasn't mine. Instead, she reached for the phone. "I am calling both your parents," she said.

"No!" cried Yasmine, genuine panic in her voice. "Please don't call my dad. Please, Miss Ward, please don't."

I was so confused then. I couldn't imagine why Miss Ward wanted to call my mom. What exactly had I done? But Miss Ward surely thought I had done something. And she was the grown-up, the one with the diplomas on her wall. She was the one in charge. So I said nothing. Instead I sat there, feeling ashamed.

"Mrs. Rawl?" Miss Ward spoke into the phone, her voice an odd combination of cheery and tight. "I am going to need you to come to school. Yes. Yes, we have a bit of a problem. Mmm-hmm. Yes, a problem with Paige and another girl. Yes. Mmm-hmm. Right away, please."

And then a short while later, we were crammed into the office, all of us: Miss Ward, Yasmine's own counselor, the assistant principal, Yasmine, Lila—they'd called her out of class, too—my mother, and Yasmine's father. Aside from Yasmine's sniffles, the occasional huffy sigh from Lila, and the *tick-tick* of the clock on the wall, it was absolutely silent in the room.

Then Miss Ward cleared her throat.

"It would seem," she said, "that these girls are having some, um, *drama*." She explained the situation, beginning with the note I hadn't written. And through my tears, I explained— again—about Yasmine's telling kids about my HIV status.

And that was how my mom learned that my HIV wasn't a secret anymore.

Her face crumpled, and I looked away.

Miss Ward handed them all copies of the note.

But I didn't write it, I wanted to scream. And I hadn't. I wouldn't. First of all, I didn't even believe what was in that note. I mean, if the invisible infection inside my blood didn't change who I was as a person, then surely her family's heritage didn't matter, either. Yasmine was just a girl. She was a girl who played the viola and piano, who loved Augustana, who liked playing pool in her great room, and who kicked a soccer ball harder than anyone I knew.

She was a kid. Like me.

Beyond that, though, there was something else. Yasmine was my friend. That's the thing: I still believed that. I couldn't help thinking that this thing that was happening to us was just a misunderstanding, crossed wires somehow. I still believed it was something we could get past. I kept feeling that if I could just do the right thing, if I could just figure out what that exact right thing was, we might somehow wind up best friends again. I thought that there might come a day when we would sit together again on the giant swing near her house, when we would return to her family's piano and play music and laugh like we used to.

If I could just figure out how to make myself clear, explain something (what? I still do not know), then everything could eventually return to normal. Perhaps that was a crazy thing to hope for. Maybe the fact that I hoped for it at all was proof that I was crazy. But I hoped for it. I believed it.

Still.

Later that night, I received an instant message from Lila.

> **Lila**: WHATS UR PROBLEM??!?? don't ever put a note in Yasmine's locker again
> **Me**: I didn't. I wouldn't do that and I don't even know what the note says
> **Lila**: I swear to GOD I WILL HIT U HARD IF U TALK TO MY SISTER AGAIN
> **Lila**: AND THAT'S NOT A THREAT
> **Lila**: THAT'S THE TRUTH

Except it *was* a threat. Anyone, even I, could see that.

I clicked off the computer. I grabbed a portable stereo and walked into the bathroom. I slammed the door, locked it behind me, then turned up music as loud as it would go. I sat down on the edge of the tub and wrapped my arms around myself, rocked back and forth.

My stomach hurt, my stupid stomach that always feels everything that happens to me.

Over the throbbing music, I heard my mom banging on the door. The banging sounded very far away, and so did her voice, calling my name. "Paige!" she shouted. "Turn that music down, honey."

And then, when I did not: "Are you okay? Paige!"

Leave me alone. Just leave me alone.

She banged and banged—"Answer me, Paige!"—until I stood up, furious. I turned down the music, just one angry flick of my wrist, and threw open the door.

"Just go away!" I screamed.

For a split second, her jaw hung open. She was stunned. I had never spoken to her like that, had never screamed right at her.

I didn't care. I couldn't care.

She swallowed. "Honey, I just wanted to make sure you're—"

"I'm fine," I snapped. "Just give me some space, will you?"

"Okay, but I just—"

I slammed the door then, right in her face, turned the music back up, and sat back down.

I realized I hated it here, in this house. I hated it at school.

I hated it absolutely everywhere.

That May, Yasmine turned twelve. Over Memorial Day weekend, she and Lila had their big party at the clubhouse, just like Yasmine and I had talked about.

I could just picture it. I imagined the streamers and balloons and silver trays of food warming over tiny flames. I imagined the *pock-pock* from the nearby tennis courts and the ripples of wind through the awnings. The temperature was in the low nineties—hot at my mother's house, but perfect for a summer party. Surely, all the kids went swimming, splashing and dunking and whooping, pool lights glowing, until late into the night.

I imagined all of that, but of course I was not there to see it. The party went on without me. It was just as if I never existed.

+ PART TWO +

Stumbling

A New Year

It is probably not every kid who can say this, but I can: there was at least one day, at the start of seventh grade, when I sat in algebra class and was 100 percent fully and completely happy.

It wasn't the algebra, of course. It's that other things were good.

Cheering for the basketball team in seventh grade—
I was so proud to have finally made the squad.

First of all, I had done it. I had made the cheerleading team. All those hours practicing with Amber, all those evenings bouncing around my own house, had paid off. Even better: not only was I on the team, but the coach had even given me roles in some of our stunts. And, wow, my uniform was the cutest thing I had ever seen: flouncy blue skirt, white trim, a tank top that said WILDCATS. I had blue-and-white ribbons for my ponytail, and blue-and-white pom-poms that rustled dreamily when I shook them.

I had spent much of the summer moping about Yasmine. I wish I hadn't done that. I wish I hadn't wasted a moment on her. But her absence from my life, her sudden and complete rejection of me, hurt. So this little victory, this whole becoming-a-cheerleader thing, the pom-poms and skirt and ribbons and all, made me feel a little victorious.

If she went to a game, after all, she wouldn't be able to avoid seeing me.

Another good thing: I had made a new friend, Mariah, who was crazy friendly and who made me laugh. She was new to Clarkstown. After we met, she told me that she had spent some time with Yasmine and some other kids over the summer. They had told her about me. They told her I had AIDS, and that she should stay away from me. But when she finally met me on the first day of school, she decided she just wasn't going to listen.

"You seemed okay to me," she said with a shrug.

I was so glad. I was glad that she wanted to hang out, glad that we might even have a sleepover this weekend. And I was especially glad when she passed me in the hallway and waved really big and called out to me loudly, as if daring anyone to say anything, "Hi, Paige!"

In case you're counting, that made Yasmine: 0, Me: 2.

There were other things, too. I had joined the Bluettes, an all-girl show choir, and Amber and I often hung out there. Our teacher, Mrs. Kay, had even told us that the Bluettes and some of the other show choir groups might get to perform in Walt Disney World. Yes, *that* Walt Disney World. The one and only.

And then there was Ethan.

Oh, my God, Ethan.

I had bumped into Ethan after my cheerleading practice the day before. He was in his soccer clothes, all sweaty in shin guards and mesh shorts. He walked toward the gym with a bunch of his teammates—Kyle Walker and Michael Jepson and a few other guys. My stomach did that fluttery thing when I saw him.

He flashed a grin and looked right at me. "Hey, Paige," he said. God, his smile was so wide and so goofy. I could have gazed at it all day. "What's up?"

Which might not sound like all that much, except here is the thing, the really important thing: he didn't keep walking toward the locker room with his buddies. He stopped. The other guys slowed down then, like maybe they would wait for him if it was only going to take a second, but when he didn't follow them, didn't even glance at them, they kept walking. He stayed.

You can imagine how fluttery I got then.

And we talked for just a minute—*How was your summer? You cheering now? Who do you have for English? Yeah, she's tough.* It didn't matter that we weren't saying much of anything at all. I would have stayed there forever saying nothing. It was enough just to stand there with him, breathing that air we shared, which I'm telling you felt different from any air I had ever breathed.

Another group of soccer players ran past us. One of them made a loud kissing noise as he passed, didn't even break his stride, and I felt my cheeks flush. I looked down at the pavement.

"Well . . . anyway," said Ethan. He sounded as embarrassed as I felt. "I should go change."

And I nodded and was about to say "See ya," when he added, kind of quickly, "We should hang out sometime."

You can laugh if you want to, but if you have ever been thirteen years old with a fluttery heart, you probably know that at that moment, I felt like I could fly.

"Yeah. Okay," I said. It was hard to look at him, but then I did. I felt my cheeks pulling my lips into a smile that no matter how hard I tried, I couldn't contain. I bit my top lip.

"So . . . okay," he said, a corner of his own mouth curling upward.

"Okay."

And we lingered just one tiny moment more, just grinning, and then he said, "I'll text you, 'kay?"

And I said, "Cool," and after he ran off, his cleats clop-clopping on the pavement beneath him, I was so happy I wanted to dance right there outside the gym.

Instead, I went home and put on my uniform and spent the rest of the evening bouncing around the house, practicing my high Vs and low Vs, right Ls and left punches. I cheered in the living room, in the kitchen. I did a split in the hallway, then leapt into a touchdown pose in the dining room. My mother watched and said it was nice to see me happy, and I stopped bouncing only when Mariah called. I took the phone into my bedroom and closed the door. I just had to tell her about Ethan.

Anyhow. I was still happy that next day, even sitting in algebra, with Mrs. Yates in the front of the classroom, droning on about square roots.

I was trying really, really hard to concentrate.

On the first day of school, Mrs. Yates had told us that if we passed this course as seventh graders, then next year, as eighth graders, we could take the bus to North City High School and take math with high school kids. She said that algebra is really just like all the math we had already learned—we would add numbers, subtract numbers, multiply, and divide. The only difference is that in algebra, one of the numbers would be a mystery.

She had showed us an example: $x + 4 = 9$, and asked, "What is x?"

It was a dumb question, because everyone was able to solve it immediately—x was 5—and I suppose that was her point. So right then, I understood that algebra is just a fancy term for using what you *do* know to figure out what you *don't* know.

So now, even though I wanted to think about Ethan and cheerleading and Disney, I was really doing my best to keep my eyes on the numbers and letters she was drawing everywhere on the board. From the corner of my eye, I saw Yasmine raise her hand.

Oh. Right. How's this for awkward? In seventh grade, Yasmine and I had five classes together. In addition to algebra, we also had English together, and social studies, and science, and we even had the same lunch period.

We were going to spend practically the whole day, every day, together.

Early on, it seemed like we had settled on an unspoken agreement: in each of these classes, we sat far apart from each other, and we refused to meet each other's eye.

Or maybe it wasn't an agreement, exactly. Maybe it was more of a competition. Which is to say, if she wasn't going to look at me, I sure as heck wasn't going to look at her.

The bell rang, and math class ended. We closed our notebooks and I went to my locker to change textbooks.

Walking toward it, I saw a note taped to my locker. I figured it was probably from Mariah. Or maybe Amber had slipped into the seventh-grade hallway on her way to gym.

Or maybe, there was always that chance, it was from Ethan.

I pulled it down eagerly. *I don't need Yasmine to have this experience*, I told myself, unfolding it. *I don't need Yasmine to get a note on my locker, to plan for sleepovers, to have friends. There are others who will leave notes for me. I have Amber and Mariah and I am a cheerleader and a Bluette and I plan to take high school math next year, when I am just in eighth grade.*

But the note was not from Mariah. It was not from Amber. The note had only four words—not even a full sentence, but those words were enough:

No AIDS at Clarkstown.

I became aware of myself standing there in the hallway, alone. Around me, kids slammed lockers, picked up books from the floor, called out to one another. They sounded happy. They seemed oblivious.

But one of those kids, at least, wasn't oblivious. Someone had singled me out.

Use what you do know to figure out what you don't.

There was so much I didn't know. I didn't know who'd left the note for me. I didn't know how many people were in on it, or how they'd learned about my HIV. And I had no idea how to change any of this.

But I did know one thing. Whatever happened last year, whatever happened between me and Yasmine, whatever happened with that stupid note she got, with the kids not wanting to drink after me, wasn't over.

I knew that being a cheerleader wouldn't be enough to make it go away, that having new friends wouldn't be enough. Maybe even having a boyfriend—if Ethan ever became that—

wouldn't be enough. I wasn't going to get a clean slate.

Instead, this thing that had been happening to me was going to keep happening. It was going to get bigger.

The bell rang, and everyone moved toward their next class. The hallway drained of kids—in groups at first, and then one by one. Everyone just kind of disappeared into classrooms until I stood alone. Those words were still right there in front of me. *No AIDS at Clarkstown.*

I had an urge to throw it, to get that note as far away from me as I could. I didn't want it, didn't want to see it, didn't want to hold it, didn't even want to touch it. But I didn't want anyone else to see it, either. I tore it up, my hands shaking. I crumpled the scraps, then brought them over to a garbage can and threw them in. I started to walk away, then turned back to the can, pushed the scraps of the note to the bottom, covering them with other kids' papers, with an energy bar wrapper, with a half-finished Snapple bottle. I bit my lip so hard I tasted blood.

If I could have figured out how to set that whole garbage can on fire, I'd have done it right then and there.

Still: I did not cry. Not yet.

I didn't cry then, and I didn't cry when I stuffed my books into the locker, and I didn't cry when I slammed the door shut. I didn't cry until I was inside the girls' bathroom, safe inside a bathroom stall.

But once I was there, I broke down.

My eyes were red-rimmed when I finally arrived, late and without a pass, to science class. There, Yasmine and I ignored each other again.

A few days later, I stood in my cheerleading uniform, blue and white, shaking pom-poms. Behind me, the Clarkstown football team ran drills, warming up for the big game against Lincoln Middle School. With just a few minutes before kickoff, the bleachers in front of me were already filled.

It was the kind of day that always made my mother sigh wistfully, say some dopey thing like "picture perfect." And even though I probably would have rolled my eyes if she'd been there to say it, I had to admit, it was a pretty nice day: sunny, warm, mild breeze, fat puffy clouds in the sky.

It was the kind of day where it seems nothing could possibly go wrong. And yet wrong things happen all the time. They happen in every kind of weather.

We cheerleaders were giving our routines one last run before the game started. We stepped out, back in again. We jumped, then kicked, placed our hands on our hips. In a just a minute, my big moment would come: three girls were going to toss me high in the air, then catch me.

The move is called a basket toss, and it made me feel like I was flying.

We stepped and turned, moved our arms into a T formation.

"Everybody do that Wildcat rumble!"

I scanned the bleachers, hoping to see Ethan. A bunch of the boys from the soccer team were in the bleachers. I figured Ethan might come soon, too.

I hoped so. I wanted Ethan there. I wanted him to see me cheer.

Step out, then in.

"Everybody do that Wildcat rumble!"

Arms in T, arms at my hips. I felt great. I was *good* at this.

That's when I heard someone in the crowd calling my name. I looked up. Some of the boys from the soccer team—Michael and Kyle and Devin—were laughing. They were laughing too hard to just be cheering for me, and as I stepped out and clap-

clap–clapped, I listened more closely.

"Paige!"

"Paige!"

For a while, I couldn't make the connection between their laughter and their calling my name.

A low V. Arms crossed over chest. High V.

Then I realized. They weren't saying my name at all. They weren't saying Paige. They were saying *PAIDS*.

"PAIDS!"

"PAIDS!"

Clap. Step. Right arm punch.

The boys' faces were pulled into wide grins, and they were doubled over laughing. Kyle noticed me looking and waved. *"Hi, PAIDS!"*

I looked away, lost my footing just a moment, then quickly fell back into step with the other girls.

Lean back, roll arms, lean forward, roll again.

Once I heard them, I could not un-hear them. And as I stepped and crossed, jumped and shouted—a smile on my face the whole time—I was intensely aware of those boys, of that name.

"Go, PAIDS!"

A whistle blew. The game would start soon.

It was like slow motion, the way the boys threw their heads back, laughing. The way they were laughing at me.

I thought about Ethan, and I instantly changed my mind. I prayed that he would not be at this game, after all. What if he heard them?

Please, God. Please, please, please don't let him come to the game today.

It was almost time for my big moment, the one where the girls would toss me into the air.

I didn't know what to do about the laughter. I was pretty sure I couldn't do anything.

Two of the girls grabbed each other's wrists, forming a square of hands. That square was the platform from which I would be tossed into the air. The girls bent down, readying themselves for me. I felt a third girl step into place behind me.

My turn.

I put my hands on the girls' shoulders and lifted myself up, standing on the base their hands had formed. The third girl gave me an extra boost from behind. Then she quickly moved her hands into place below the others'—an extra bit of support, just in case.

This all happened in a few seconds.

It was important to concentrate. It was important to pretend that none of the other stuff was happening, that nobody was making fun of me, that the smiles in the bleachers weren't terribly twisted. I just really, really needed to concentrate.

I have done this before, I told myself. *I have practiced it so many times.* I placed all my weight onto my arms, balanced myself on their shoulders, my feet still resting on their interlocked hands.

The girls bent their knees, and I felt myself being lowered into position.

Here. We. Go.

We had only a second, and precision was everything.

Then, in an instant, it happened. The girls sprang up straight and pushed up with their arms, releasing me into the air. At the exact moment, I used my arms to power myself off their shoulders with every bit of strength I had.

It happened: I flew.

All I needed now was get into a pike position—stretch both legs out in front of me, knees locked. Then I would fall back into their arms. The two girls at my side would catch my legs with their arms, and the girl behind me would gently catch my head and neck, and just like that, I would be lowered safely back to earth.

It all looks so light and so effortless when you do it right.

"PAIDS!"

And perhaps it was because I heard that name and failed to pike correctly. Or maybe it was that the girl behind me, the one who was supposed to catch my head and neck, was distracted, too. Or maybe it was as simple as this: sometimes one bad thing follows another bad thing, even on a sunny, picture perfect kind of day. Whatever it was, something went wrong.

I felt it almost instantly. Something went terribly wrong.

I felt hands catch my legs, but something else was wrong. My head was in the wrong place. It was closer to the ground than it should have been, and my whole body was tilting backward. My head angled toward the earth.

It couldn't have been more than a fraction of a second, but it was long enough to register this thought: *This is bad.* Out of pure instinct, I tucked my head toward my neck, away from the ground.

There was a loud crack as my back hit the ground.

It is a strange thing when you find yourself unexpectedly helpless on the ground. It takes a few moments to reorient yourself. A person becomes so accustomed to looking straight out at the world, to seeing only those things that fall into narrow space that is our normal field of vision—faces and blackboards and GIRLS signs on bathroom doors and EMPLOYEE OF THE MONTH plaques in fast-food joints. But suddenly, when you're least expecting it, those things give way to other things—clouds, blue sky, a tiny jet plane overhead. Then faces at all the wrong angles, a little circle of faces crowding above you and saying, *"Paige, Paige, are you okay?"*

And that's when you become aware of other things—the commotion in the stands, the murmurs of *"Is she okay?"* and *"Heard her head hit"* and *". . . maybe has a concussion."*

And also the pain. My back hurt so much I wanted to puke.

I tried to stand up, but someone pushed me down, and said, "No, don't move."

The school nurse came over, looked at my eyes, asked me where it hurt. I was still flat on my back. Then she directed people—some group of people, God only knows who—to lift me up and transport me outside the chain-link fence that borders the football field.

They got me out of sight, I suppose, out of the way of the crowds, making it possible to see me only if someone turned around and really watched.

The whistle blew. The game on the other side of the fence began. Somebody must have called an ambulance, because a little while later I heard a siren—distant, at first, then getting closer, and then suddenly there it was, lights flashing. It backed into place, and all the while I was just lying there, the world blurry on the other side of tears.

If you are wondering whether I was crying from pain or shame or disappointment, the answer is *yes*.

Strangers in black—EMTs, I guess—lifted me onto a stretcher, and loaded me, headfirst, into the ambulance.

As I disappeared into the vehicle, I saw two things. First, against the afternoon light, I saw the silhouettes of Kyle, Michael, and Devin, still high in the bleachers. They weren't watching the field. Their shoulders were still rounded, the shape of boys who are totally relaxed and at ease. They were half turned in their seats. I knew they were watching me go.

I turned away from them then, turned my head in the opposite direction. There, I caught a brief glimpse of Ethan.

He stood there, totally expressionless, his eyes on me, on this whole horrifying scene.

The doors closed behind me, and Clarkstown disappeared.

I wished it would disappear forever.

Don't Let Them Get to You

When you have HIV, you get used to people paying extraclose attention to your health. A cold is never just a cold the way it is for other kids—there's always that worry that HIV has killed off enough immune cells that it will be harder to heal. That's why my mother watches me closely and asks me constantly how I feel. When a fever comes along, she often calls the doctor. I've gotten used to that by now.

I missed a few days of school after my cheerleading fall—I was sore, with a bruise on my back, but otherwise okay. The school sent a poster-sized card to my house that had been signed by a whole bunch of kids. I scanned the names and saw the names Michael Jepson, Kyle Walker, and Devin Holt.

"Throw it away," I told my mom. When she asked why, I left the room, went into my bedroom, and slammed the door.

I didn't want to go back, I didn't want to go back, I didn't want to go back. But I was in seventh grade. When you're in seventh grade, you have to go back.

Then, a few weeks after returning to classes, I missed a few more days of school. It was nothing at all—a sinus infection, runny nose, headache, mild fever. It could have happened to anyone.

Honestly.

But when I returned to school, I noticed that kids moved around me in a wide arc as they passed in the hallway.

Pulling books out of my locker, I noticed a group of girls

watching me, speaking quietly to one another. They weren't even trying to pretend to look away. They stood there, staring. They looked totally indifferent.

I remembered Amber snapping at us on the day of the Colts parade. *Can I help you?* she had barked. I tried to imagine myself saying that to these girls, being feral like Amber. I couldn't picture myself doing that. I placed my books neatly in my bag, feeling a bit like an animal in a zoo.

"What the heck is with everyone?" I muttered.

Mariah sighed. "Yasmine told kids that you were, like, really sick."

I shut my locker. "Arrgh," I growled. "She's just so . . ." I couldn't even finish the sentence.

I mean, okay, Yasmine had made it crystal clear that we weren't friends anymore. But if we weren't friends, couldn't she just leave it at that? Why did she have to go and talk about me, too?

That's when a kid I barely knew—a chubby boy in a gray T-shirt, who wasn't even in any of my classes, came up to me.

"Is it true?" he asked. "Are you actually dying now?"

"It was just a sinus infection," I said. I frowned. "Everyone gets sinus infections."

"Can you back off, please?" said Mariah to the boy.

He shrugged. "Whatever you say . . ." And I could tell he did not believe me.

As he walked away, Mariah said to me, "It's pretty bad, actually, how much people are talking about you. You should tell someone. Miss Fischer, maybe. Or Miss Ward."

"Maybe." I thought about the last time I saw Miss Ward. I thought about sitting there waiting for my mom in Miss Ward's office, looking at her bright red fingernails.

"Paige, they can't help you if they don't know what's going

on," said Mariah. "You know?"

"I guess," I said.

So I knocked on Miss Ward's door. For the second time, I sat down in her chair. Miss Ward folded her hands on her desk and blinked at me with her mascaraed lashes.

"Paige," she said. "What brings you to see me today?"

I told her about what was said during my absence. I told her about the note—*No AIDS at Clarkstown.* I told her about the instant messages Lila had sent me at home, about my new nickname, PAIDS. I told her that Yasmine, my former best friend, even told other kids—she told Mariah at least—not to be friends with me.

I told her I felt like I was walking through a minefield. Miss Ward looked at me blankly, so I tried to explain: it wasn't so much that I was being bullied twenty-four hours a day, seven days a week. It's that I was constantly afraid that at any moment, everything might suddenly go wrong. That some new passing comment, some new note would appear out of the blue. I told her I was starting to feel frozen in place, that I dreaded school—that every day, my stomach hurt as I got ready. That Clarkstown was beginning to feel like hostile territory.

I told her that this was new, that I'd never felt like this about school before.

I told her I just didn't know what to do.

I genuinely wanted her to help me. I wanted her tell me how to make this better, how to make it go away. I wanted her to say something like: *Okay, I will take care of things,* so I could just know that it would be over.

But instead, Miss Ward just sat there. She didn't say anything for a long time, and when she did, her words were not what I expected.

"Paige," she said. "I think this is enough drama, don't you?"

Her words were so different from what I thought they would be that for a moment I didn't understand what she was saying. She must have thought it was obvious, though, because she did not offer any more explanation.

I sat. I waited.

"You know, Yasmine is a straight-A student," she said.

Again, this was not what I expected. I turned these words over in my mind. *Yasmine is a straight-A student.*

So am I, I thought. But I didn't dare say it. Instead, I just looked down.

She shook her head sadly. "Yasmine could have been a good friend, you know."

I blinked, looking at my own hands in my lap. I realized they were folded, just like hers. I unfolded them. *She could have been a good friend.* What did that even mean? She could have been, sure. If . . . what? What was the end of that sentence? If I hadn't had HIV? If she were a better person? If I were?

"This is your warning," Miss Ward said. I could hear the displeasure in her voice. "Do you understand?"

I nodded, even though I didn't.

For just an instant, I tried to see what Miss Ward saw when she looked at me. This woman had hundreds of kids coming in and out of her office. My mom was probably correct—many of them were the kids who got in trouble. To Miss Ward, Yasmine probably looked like a model student. I mean, Yasmine got straight As. She played the viola, she played sports. She came from a hardworking academic family.

If I was complaining about Yasmine, who was better behaved than most of the kids Miss Ward saw, then surely *I* was the problem. *I* must be seeking drama.

I even dared to ask the question of myself. *Was* I just being dramatic?

Almost instantly, the answer came back to me.

No. This wasn't drama.

It wasn't drama, because this was something that could defeat me completely. I don't know how I knew that, but I did. This thing, whatever happened, could kill me if I let it.

I had no idea how to make that clear.

"Thank you, Paige," Miss Ward said. "You may return to class."

I stood up and walked to the door.

"Thank you," I said. And of all the things I wish I'd done differently—all the moments of that time that I've since replayed in my mind—those two little words are among the things I most regret. *Thank you.*

Maybe Miss Ward didn't mean it this way, but here is what I took from that: my reporting incidents was the problem. That my telling her what was happening to me was causing drama. For her, I guess. And that I had to stop.

I had to stop reporting incidents.

By now, it was clear that everyone knew about my HIV. I could tell by the way kids sometimes shoved their friends into me as a joke, as if we were in second grade and I was the girl with cooties. I could tell by the whispers—". . . the girl with AIDS . . . don't touch her"—in the hallway.

One afternoon, I walked into show choir rehearsal. Our trip to Walt Disney World was getting closer and closer, and we spent our practices getting ready. Mrs. Kay was at the piano working with some of the boys from the 73rd Street singers. Michael and Kyle were among them. They sounded pretty good, actually. The other kids, including the Bluettes, were sprawled out all over the stage.

As I approached the stage, one of the eighth-grade girls grinned at me. Molly was blond and blue-eyed, a member of the student council, the kind of kid that any parent would've been thrilled to have their own daughter be friends with. *A nice girl*, they'd say about her. *Molly's such a nice girl.*

Except hers was not a nice grin at all. It was a mean-girl kind of grin.

"Well, hiiiii, Paige," she said, drawing out each word. Around her, a bunch of girls started snickering.

"Hi," I said quickly. I looked away.

Molly glanced at the girls and turned back to me. "So how are—"

But before she could get one more word out, Amber stood up. "If you're just saying hi to her to entertain your bitch friends, then you better shut your mouth." Amber stepped closer to Molly, so close that Molly took a step backward. "Paige doesn't care about you, and neither do I."

The girl glanced quickly at her friends. The room was silent now. Even Mrs. Kay looked up from across the room. I felt Michael's and Kyle's eyes on me, too.

"No response, huh?" Amber asked. Her voice dripped with disdain. She shook her head. "Fuck you, Molly."

"Amber." Mrs. Kay's voice was sharp.

"What?" Amber flashed her eyes at Mrs. Kay. She was in fighting mode now.

"We don't use language like that at Clarkstown."

"Okay, Mrs. Kay," she said. "What *the hell* ever."

"Amber . . ." A last-warning voice now from Mrs. Kay.

"Yes, Mrs. Kay," Amber said, quieter now. "Okay, sorry."

And then under her breath, to me she whispered, "Totally worth it."

I smiled at Amber and tried to ignore the fact that everyone in the room was staring at me.

I sat down and pulled out my phone. I started texting Mariah, *How are you*, not because I had anything I particularly wanted to say to her, but instead just to have somewhere to look other than around this room, with all these eyes staring at me.

After rehearsal, I walked out into the hall with Amber.

"Thanks for before," I said.

She made a face. "I just can't stand people when people are two-faced, you know? I mean if you don't want to be friends with someone, don't be friends with them. But don't talk shit about them and then try to make people laugh by saying hi to them like you're best friends."

I let that sink in. "They've been talking about me?"

Amber shrugged. "You know what I mean."

I guessed I did.

We walked silently for a bit, and then I took a deep breath. "Amber?" I asked. "Are you ever embarrassed about your mom?"

She stopped walking and looked at me—I worried she might be angry, but instead she just looked surprised. "You mean about her MS?"

"I guess," I said.

"Hell no," she said, and she started walking again. I could tell by her voice that she really meant it. "My mom's my mom. She didn't do anything wrong."

Then, after a pause, she added quietly, "She gets embarrassed, though. I tell her she shouldn't, that she can't help it, but you know how it is."

I nodded. I did know. I knew exactly.

"Anyway," she said. "Paige, just don't let those idiots bother you, okay?"

"I won't," I said, and I stuck my chin out as if to prove I wouldn't.

And I was trying. I really was trying. I was doing my homework and practicing my cheerleading jumps and smiling as I walked in the hallway, just as I imagined a seventh-grade cheerleader was supposed to. And on weekends, Mariah and I painted our toenails, and we tied ridiculous ponytails all around our heads, and we laughed and laughed and then ate cheese puffs from the bag while watching television. And I smiled at Ethan when I passed him in the hallway, and we even texted sometimes in the evening—*What are you doing? Homework, you?*—and I let my mother hand me pudding cups and remind me to take my medicine, and we still sometimes sang country songs on karaoke, and on the surface, it all looked so normal.

I swear, I was doing everything I could do to keep it normal. I was doing everything I could to keep those kids from bothering me.

But the next day, as I walked into the cafeteria, a boy came up to me, walked right up to my face, and said, "Hi, PAIDS," and I just wanted to crawl into a hole.

He stood there grinning at me. It was like he was daring me to do something about it, to say something in return. Or maybe he just wanted to prove to me that he could do this, that he had this power, and that I lacked the power to stop it.

I wanted to say something, to shout something, but didn't know what to say. Just like I didn't know what to say when I heard "PAIDS" in the hallway, "PAIDS" as I walked to science, "PAIDS" by the lockers, in the gym, sitting down in math class.

Amber would have known how to respond. Amber would have said something like, "Hello to you, too, ass-hat." Or she would have taken one step toward him and said, "Do you really want to do this now?" And I swear it would have been enough to make him step back nervously. Or she would have said, "Just get the fuck out of here," and he would have.

She would have done *something*, anyway, something more than blink and turn away, pretending she hadn't heard a thing.

Which, of course, is exactly what I did.

That night, I lay in bed and thought about names. I tried to think of any other name that could be morphed into the word AIDS. I even went online and looked at names.

There were none. They could have only done it with the name Paige.

It's like I was destined to be this, somehow. Destined to be PAIDS.

That boy was right. I was powerless to stop it, powerless to stop any of this, the way it was all falling apart. All of it, so swiftly falling apart.

Just Go

"So, why pageants?" Ethan asked.

We were at Ethan's house, on the sofa in his family room. His mom and brother were somewhere in the house, but right now, this moment, it was just him and me.

We were playing video games. Basketball, of course.

He was better at it than I was, which I guess was no surprise. I kept getting distracted by the crowds that were built into the game, by the commentary, by the high kicks of the video game cheerleaders.

My player dribbled slowly, turned, and looked for someone to pass the ball to.

Ethan moved a player past me; the player stole the ball as he passed.

"Jerk," I said.

"Sorry," he laughed. His eyes focused on the flat screen that hung on the wall. His player dribbled right down the center of the court, making an easy layup.

"Twenty-seven to eight," he said, not looking at me.

"Shut up," I said.

My phone hummed. I picked it up. It was a text from my mom. *Everything ok?*

"Oh, my God, my mother."

I texted back. *Yeah fine. Playing video games.*

I turned back to Ethan.

"So what were we talking about?" I asked.

"Pageants." His eyes were still fixed on the game.

"You don't really care about pageants."

Another text from my mom. *Who is winning?*

"I'm curious," he said.

I texted back. *He is. Gotta go.*

"Okay, so what was the question?"

"I don't know. What are they like?"

"They're fun. You get to dress up. You meet lots of other girls."

He tossed a three-point shot, and the crowd on his side of the court went wild. A band started up and his fans stood up and cheered, rolling their fists in the air.

"Do you win money?" he asked.

"Not usually. I just like doing them."

"Because you dress up?"

"Well . . ."

It was a hard thing to explain. I loved so many things about pageants. I loved the patter and bustle of girls backstage, the laughter as we zipped ourselves into gowns, or ran a brush through our hair one last time. I loved watching Heather—she and I were good friends now—apply makeup, so carefully that you couldn't see the makeup itself. Instead, you only noticed features that you might not have seen before, like the sparkle in her eyes, or her high, elegant forehead. I still was not allowed to wear makeup in my age division, but when I did start wearing it, I planned to wear it exactly the way Heather did.

I loved meeting other girls from around the state, from so many different backgrounds. Some girls came from unimaginably hard situations, and you could just hear their determination when they answered judges' questions. *"I plan to attend medical school." "I plan to be a talk show host." "I'm going to help children whose dads were injured while serving our nation, like my own dad was."*

I loved those girls especially, the ones with plans.

I loved the flurry and excitement of it all, the nervous butterflies that appeared as we all waited backstage, then the instant calm that came over me as I stepped onto the stage into the lights. I loved being with my mom while getting ready, then later, knowing she was out there in the darkness, silently rooting for me.

I loved the way pageants helped me feel so *in control*—of myself, of what happened next, of my own destiny. I loved the way they made me feel so confident, when so many other things made me feel the opposite.

I looked at Ethan now and shrugged. "Well, why do you like basketball?"

"I like shooting baskets."

"That's it?"

He smiled, his face still on the screen. "That's not enough?"

"Okay, then. I don't know why I like pageants. I like everything, I guess."

A small face appeared in the room. His little brother. "Get out, Jake," Ethan said in a warning voice. The face disappeared.

Ethan shouted, "Seriously! Go!" We heard the sound of footsteps running down the stairs.

"So you like everything," he said.

"Yeah, pretty much."

He took a three-point shot, sunk it, and paused the game. He looked at me. "Do you have pictures?"

"Oh, God, my mom takes so many pictures."

"You should post them."

"Like online?"

"No, like on a billboard, dummy." He nudged his foot against my leg. "Of course, online."

I laughed. But he left his foot there, right on my leg.

I wasn't thinking about pageants then.

And that's when Ethan leaned over toward me. His face was right next to mine. And then he came even closer, and then his face was touching mine. He kissed me. His mom was moving around in the kitchen just one room away, and his lips were on my lips, and it was wonderful.

We heard a noise in the doorway and looked up. His brother, Jake, again. Ethan threw a pillow at him, and the boy disappeared. We looked at each other and laughed, and he did not move his foot from my leg.

"You really should post a picture, you know," he said, his eyes locked on mine.

God, I was happy then. I was so happy exactly like that, on the couch.

"Yeah, maybe I will."

So I did. I did it that very night. I wanted to think about how Ethan grinned at me on the sofa, the way his foot nudged me. I wanted to think about his wide, goofy smile, and the way he was so embarrassed when I saw his baby picture by the door when it was time for my mother to pick me up.

I wanted to think about that kiss. Over and over and over again.

I uploaded photos, some of my favorite ones, then I walked away from the computer for a while to do math homework—Mrs. Yates was really getting on my case these days. And then I finished my homework, finished dinner, and even read some of Anne Frank's diary, even though that was the last thing I wanted to read about. I returned to the computer, wondering if he might have sent me a message.

He hadn't. But beneath one of the photos, there was a short comment from a girl who went to another school. I barely even knew her; the girl's sister and I were once in an academic after-school program together. Both of them had always seemed really nice, super friendly. They lived in a big white house with columns on the porch and carefully trimmed hedges along the sidewalk. A nice family, most people would say. Nice girls.

She had left me this message. She had sought me out, looked for my online profile, even though she barely knew me.

Because there on my photo, this girl who I barely knew, this girl who attended a different school entirely, had left a comment, one I didn't even entirely understand:

you look like an aids baby mama.

I looked at those words for a long time. It was like wolves circling or something, this situation. It started with just a few, but more and more animals were circling now. I stood up and went to the bathroom, slammed the door, and put on music. I turned on the shower but did not get in. Instead, I sat on the floor and rocked back and forth.

Just breathe.

I rocked for a long time. I rocked until the mirror became steamed up, then even longer. Drops of water rolled down the mirror, leaving clear streaks. I rocked until the throbbing music was all there was. Then I got up and went back into my room, lay down on the covers.

A moment later, my mom knocked on my door.

"Paige?"

I just lay there.

"Paige," she said. She opened the door a little and stood in the doorway. "Heather's mom says that Heather's signing up for the National American Miss pageant. She's doing the junior teen division. You could do the preteen division."

I didn't answer.

"You and Heather could do it together."

I moaned.

She walked over and sat down on the bed. "You should do it. It'll be fun."

I sat up then. Suddenly, I was furious. I was furious at my mother for coming in here, furious for her wanting me to do anything, furious for suggesting that anything would be fun, ever.

"Just get out," I screamed.

"Oh, honey, what's the—"

"I don't want to do your stupid pageant."

"Well, it's not my—"

"You just want me to walk around and smile as if everything's okay. You want me to smile and wave and wear pretty dresses so that you can tell yourself that everything's just fine. But it's not fine, and it's never going to be fine, and so I don't want to tell you that it is, just so *you'll* feel better." I grabbed the paper in her hand and ripped it away from her. Her eyes widened.

I crumpled it just enough to throw it, and I hurled it across the room.

"Paige, that's not why I want you to—"

"Just go away, Mom." I was pleading now, my face screwing up into a cry. "Just get out and go away and don't talk to me about pageants anymore. Please, Mom. Please, just go."

She stood up and looked at me with such concern, such sadness, I couldn't bear it. I turned away from her.

"I just don't know what to do, Paige."

"Please, Mom. Please. The best thing you can do is just go."

She did not move for a long time.

"Please go, Mom."

"Okay," she said. I felt her get off the bed and heard her pick up the crumpled paper. She left the room and shut the door carefully behind her as she left.

I lay there and did not move.

Ugly

Today, when I look through my middle school yearbooks, I have trouble connecting what I see on those pages with the hard tight feeling that comes over me whenever I think about Clarkstown. In those yearbooks, in color photos, are smiling, friendly faces, doing all the things kids are supposed to do. There are kids blowing into trumpets, slamming tennis balls with rackets, singing in costume at the center of a spotlight. There are kids walking in groups, arms draped around one another casually, giving an invisible photographer the thumbs-up sign. There are kids in football helmets, kids with hands raised in the classroom, kids grinning as they stroll, relaxed, into the gymnasium. These kids, all of them, look so at ease, so happy.

Maybe most of them genuinely were.

But the thing is, I keep seeing myself in these pages. In one photo, I'm standing in a cheerleading outfit, my blue-and-white Wildcats pom-poms placed confidently on my hips. In another, I'm surrounded by a crush of about twenty kids at a basketball game; everyone appears to be either laughing or hollering with glee. In all these photos, I'm smiling.

I look, in all honesty, happy.

And maybe that's what Miss Ward saw, and my teachers, too. Perhaps that's why they dismissed my pleas for help, made up their minds that my complaints were nothing more than the usual drama of early adolescent friendships. Maybe they saw a kid who was friendly and bubbly, who cheered her heart out at basketball games, who surrounded herself with other kids, who seemed to love being a part of things. Maybe they thought that those things, those things alone, told them everything they needed to know.

Maybe they really believed that the things they saw mattered far more than the words that were coming out of my mouth.

But I'm not so sure.

And the reason I'm not sure has everything to do with the history of HIV and AIDS.

In 1981, doctors began noticing surprising numbers of men affected by a rare cancer, Kaposi's sarcoma, as well as a weird type of pneumonia, *Pneumocystis carinii pneumonia* (PCP). It didn't make sense: the men who had gotten these diseases were young and had been in good health. We know now that these were just opportunistic infections—infections that had taken hold only because the men's immune systems were so weakened. We know that the real cause of *that* was the HIV virus. But at the time, it was all a mystery. The *New York Times* reported on the rise of Kaposi's sarcoma, noting that 20 percent of the men who had gotten it had died within two years of being diagnosed.

Oh, yeah, and the newspaper reported that all the infected men happened to be gay.

It was a different time in US history. Back then, there were virtually no openly gay celebrities. No openly gay actors, singers, talk show hosts, musicians . . . and certainly no openly gay politicians. The same year, it was reported that Billie Jean King, a widely beloved professional tennis player, was gay. She lost every endorsement she had. In every state in America, it was still legal to discriminate against someone based on his/her sexual orientation. In many states, being gay itself was a crime. Homosexuality was considered a mental illness by members of the medical community; it was years before doctors would remove sexual orientation from the *Diagnostic and Statistical Manual of Mental Disorders*, the standard-bearer of the psychiatric industry.

News of a "gay cancer" spread rapidly. By the end of 1981, there was almost a new case being diagnosed every single day. And although by mid-1982 the disease started showing up in heterosexual men and women, that did little to destigmatize the disease. Nearly all those straight men and women were intravenous drug users who had gotten the disease from sharing needles.

So that's how the disease was discovered in the United States: in gay men and in drug users. Not exactly the most stigma-free populations.

There was such disgrace in an AIDS diagnosis that no one— even the doctors who treated the disease—was immune to it. Caregivers who treated AIDS patients were sometimes shunned by their peers. Dr. Joel Weisman, one of the first AIDS physicians, once wrote about a conversation with a fellow physician. The other doctor, said Joel, declared that if AIDS were to "kill a few of them off"—meaning gays, I guess, or drug addicts, or anyone else who happened to get the disease—"it will make society a better place."

For a long time, I didn't know any of that; I still thought HIV was like any other disease. I knew people with diabetes. I knew people with arthritis. I knew people with high blood pressure and eczema and cavities and farsightedness. Perhaps if I'd understood that HIV had originally been seen—unlike those other conditions—as a disease of outcasts, I wouldn't have been as confused by people's reactions to me.

. . .

I had been a good girl, mind you. I had done what the adults told me. I had let that last meeting with Miss Ward be my final one.

No more drama.

My mom, though, was worried. She left messages for Miss Fischer. She stopped by the school to see her. She left a note in Miss Fischer's office, handing it to the school secretary with the words, "Please make sure she gets this."

Mom followed up with phone calls. She never got a call back.

It's possible the administrators somehow never got those messages. Or maybe they simply didn't know what to do.

But sometimes I wonder if the problem was HIV itself. These administrators surely remembered those early days, when AIDS had been seen as a telltale sign of depravity, of someone who is less worthy than others. What if they carried some of those old prejudices, even unconsciously? What if the fact that I had HIV was enough to put me, or my mom, in a new category in their eyes?

What if they heard HIV and thought only of those at the margins of polite society?

Yasmine's a straight-A student. (As if I wasn't.)

She could have been a good friend. (Except she wasn't.)

You can just deny that you have HIV. (Except I did have it.)

I recalled the time in sixth grade when I got in trouble for laughing in the hall, when I had to write an essay about why I shouldn't be suspended. It didn't make any sense: laughter was an offense worth suspending a kid over, but telling the school that I had HIV wasn't? Calling someone "PAIDS" wasn't?

I imagined Yasmine imitating Miss Fischer: *I am the very proud principal of a school where laughing might get you suspended. But making up hurtful nicknames gets you a starting place on the basketball team.*

When I imagined that, I laughed out loud, even though I was all alone in my bedroom. I laughed like a crazy person.

In fact, the whole situation made me feel like I was crazy, like a little part of me had gone completely nuts.

Mostly, it made me feel desperately alone.

By midyear, my grades had begun to plummet. I began missing school—a lot of it. I forgot assignments, lost homework. Sometimes I read over the same paragraph six or seven times, and still couldn't remember what it said. My stomach hurt constantly.

Mrs. Yates, my algebra teacher, had grown particularly impatient with me. "You either do the work, or you don't," she said simply when I tried to explain what was happening with me.

"I'll do the work," I said, even though the numbers had long since stopped making any sense. All of those x's and y's and parentheses and sweeping angles on grids . . . they all required so much concentration.

I'll try, I would tell myself. *If I can just make myself focus, keep my eyes on the page, stop my mind from wandering, I can do this.*

And then, when I didn't turn in my next homework assignment, Mrs. Yates said, "Without a doctor's note, you will not pass this course."

I went to see Dr. Cox. She checked my vital signs, pressed down on my belly.

"Hmm," she said. "How's everything going, Paige?"

And I wanted to tell her.

I used to love going to school, I wanted to say. *I used to love it, but then something changed.*

I wanted to tell her how it felt the other night when I went out for smoothies with Mariah, and some girls I didn't even know were whispering about me. I heard them say "AIDS" and "slut," and I felt so ashamed. I wanted to tell her that I got a phone call recently from Yasmine, Madison, and Lila. I heard their voices over the phone. "You're ugly," I heard them say. "You're too ugly to be in pageants."

The three of them, my old friends, were all together. It wasn't so long ago that we had been a foursome. And now I was just standing there, listening to them. I was trying to move on—God, I was trying so hard—but instead all I could do was hold the phone, picturing them all together.

I don't understand what is happening to me, I wanted to tell Dr. Cox. I didn't know why I found myself shaking sometimes, why I woke up in the middle of the night grinding my teeth and then could not fall back asleep. I didn't know why I couldn't seem to keep my eyes on my math workbook, why my head seemed to hurt all the time.

Dr. Cox watched me closely, waiting for my answer.

"It's going okay," I said. I shrugged and did not meet her eye. I knew it could be so much worse. No one was pushing me down stairs or pulling my hair. I knew that happened sometimes when kids got bullied.

Sticks and stones may break my bones, but names will never hurt me.

I'm rubber, you're glue.

There was something wrong with me if I let their words hurt me, and I knew it.

"Paige?" Dr. Cox asked more softly.

And then her office was swimming. My eyes filled with tears. I could not hold them back anymore. They came streaming out of me, even as I sat there saying, "I'm okay. I'm okay. I swear, I'm really okay."

. . .

A few days later, I was back in the bathroom again, music blasting. Rocking back and forth, back and forth.

In my hand was another note. Another one.

I'd seen my name on the bathroom wall today. *PAIGE HAS AIDS. Slut. Go home.*

And in my hands was this scrap of paper, which I'd found tucked into a notebook. It was torn from a spiral notebook, the edge still frayed.

Four words. Different words from the last note.

You bitch. You hoe.

Sitting there in the bathroom, I wasn't paying attention to the music. I wasn't thinking about school.

I was aware of that note, and of one other thing.

I was aware of my mom's nail scissors, those tiny steel nail scissors with the sharp tip, which were in the top drawer.

I want to get the scissors I want to hold them I want to feel the steel, scrape the blade against my skin.

My wrists. I longed to put those scissors on my wrists.

I realized I had been longing for that for a while, the feel of steel on skin.

I rocked and rocked, tried concentrating on the chorus of the song. *I hope you know, I hope you know that this has nothing to do with you, it's personal, myself and I, we've got some straightenin' out to do. . . .*

But oh, my God, those scissors. The steel. The sharp edges.

Something was so wrong with me. It was so wrong, I knew, that I couldn't stop thinking about them.

My mother was on the other side of the wall. I tried to think of what she would tell me right now if she knew what I was thinking about. I couldn't imagine it. I couldn't imagine her knowing, couldn't even begin to think how she would react if she knew what I wanted to do.

I pictured Dr. Cox's face, that look of concern she gave me the last time I was in her office. I felt so bad when I'd told her about everything, like I'd let her down.

She had taken such good care of me for so many years. I owed it to her to be happier, to live the life that she had been trying to keep me alive for.

The scissors the scissors the scissors.

I looked again at the crumpled paper in my hands. I squeezed into a ball. My body shook.

And then, just like that, I had the strangest sensation. It was as if none of this was real. Not the lined, frayed-edge note in my hand, or the scrawl in ball-point pen. Not the music around me, not the fluorescent light overhead.

Not even me. Even I wasn't real—it was like I was watching myself from far away, watching a movie of a girl who couldn't stop thinking about scissors and wrists.

I felt an instant calm.

I stood up and snapped off the radio, carried the note into my bedroom. I tore it into pieces, wrapped the pieces in a tissue, and threw the whole thing away. Then I lay down flat on my bed, arms and legs straight by my side.

My pageant crowns were on my dresser. My book bag lay on the floor.

I watched myself lying there. I did not move.

First Seizure

And then. Basketball season.

We cheerleaders had just changed into our uniforms. Most of the other girls were leaving the locker room, but I sat there on the bench. My stomach hurt.

Amber turned around as she went out the door. "Come on, Paige," she called out. "Hurry up!"

I stood up, followed her up the gym stairs, my blue Wildcats skirt brushing my legs. The crowd in the bleachers was a sea of blue and white—students and teachers, parents and brothers and sisters and community members. So many of them, come to cheer on the team.

I couldn't see my mom in the crowd.

My stomach. Oh, God, my stomach. I didn't know if I was getting sick. I hoped not. The show choir trip to Walt Disney World was coming up soon. I could never go feeling like this.

The basketball team warmed up, each player taking turns with one layup after another. Kyle Walker ran toward the basket, sank one easily, and then passed the ball to Michael Jepson.

Michael Jepson. *A good guy.* It's what everyone said.

People were still arriving at the gym, still buying their tickets on the other side of the double doors.

I craned my head to see if my mom was arriving, but I couldn't see her.

On the far wall, above the basket, there was a wildcat face painted in blue. Its mouth was open in a roar. Closer to me was the scoreboard, the American flag.

Shoes squeaked on the wooden gym floor.

The referee blew the whistle, and we took our places: feet wide, arms behind our back. We were ready.

Amber was right in front of me. I saw her, saw the crowd. I heard the noise. And that's when it happened.

I felt a burst of heat in the middle of my body, felt it rush outward, all through me. Then, almost immediately, I felt a cold breeze, and I realized I was sweating. I started shaking then, really shaking, and it occurred to me my knees were weak, too weak to support my body.

How had these knees ever supported me?

Amber turned around to say something to me, but by that point, I could not hear her.

The world turned greenish gray, and all the commotion of the gym—the crowds, the whistle—got very far away. Amber narrowed her eyes and stepped toward me.

And that's the last thing I remember. She just disappeared.

Everything in the world—the world itself—disappeared.

It really does happen that way. One minute, you're looking at a painted wildcat face on a cinder-block wall, and everything is loud around you. And then the next thing you know, you are in a bed inside the emergency room, and someone has placed sticky things all over your chest, and these sticky things connect to wires, which connect to a machine that beeps and has lights.

I recognized Riley immediately.

Amber was by my side, along with my mother.

I had no idea how much time had passed.

God, my mother's face was such a mess—it was blotchy and red, and there were tears rolling down her cheeks and clear fluid at the base of her nose. She must have wiped her nose, because there was a glistening horizontal streak across her cheek.

I blinked a couple of times. "What happened?"

My mother shook her head. "You had a seizure."

"You scared me to death," said Amber. "That's what happened."

Okay, I thought. *That explains something.* I had been in the gym. And now I was here, and in between there was a seizure. But why—?

"Amber rode in the ambulance with you," said my mom.

"They told me I wasn't allowed to, but I got in anyway," said Amber.

My mom reached over and put one of her hands on Amber's.

"And then Amber insisted on being in the emergency room with you the whole time." She turned to look at Amber. "I still have no idea how you got away with that."

Amber shrugged. "I said, 'What, you're gonna leave a thirteen-year-old girl alone in a hallway in a hospital in the middle of downtown?' They didn't have any answer to that."

My mother beamed at Amber. "She's been a really good friend."

"But why did I—?" I asked.

"We don't know yet, Paige," Mom said. "But you're stable now. That's what matters."

Doctors ran tests. Blood work. Heart monitors. They looked at my eyes and asked me to move fingers and toes. They asked me if I recognized my mother, how old I was, what year it was. They put me inside a loud tube and made me lie perfectly still so they could take pictures of my brain. They made me stand with my eyes shut, made me squeeze fingers.

Then eventually, they sent me home.

Amber came home with us that night. My mom heated up

some soup, and the two of them sat together in the kitchen as I crawled into bed. Then Amber spent the night in my room as I slept—"Just in case, Mrs. Rawl"—and she did not sleep at all.

In the morning, Amber went to school, and I went back to the doctors, where they told me what went wrong.

It was both a relief and not a relief, because nothing was wrong and everything was.

At the end of the day, when Amber showed up back at the house, I told her what the doctors had said. I told her the medical name for my diagnosis—psychogenic non-epileptic seizures—as well as the nickname. *Pseudoseizures.*

I told her what else we learned: that what happened to me in the gym is something that happens sometimes to returning war veterans, to mothers in child-custody battles, to anyone who is overextended, too deeply stressed for too long.

Amber was silent for a long time after I told her that.

"Well, fuck," she finally said. "I didn't know it had gotten that bad."

Not Tell Them

And then we went to Walt Disney World, we flew halfway across the country to sing in the Magic Kingdom, and it was supposed to be so amazing.

And it was—at first.

The night before we left for the airport, Amber spent the night at my house. We woke up early, completely giddy—*"It's finally heeeere,"* said Amber when my clock radio went off. My room was still dark, the shades still drawn, and I whispered in response, *"Yessss."* We got ready together. (Straightening iron on my hair, loose ponytail for Amber. The gray hoodie for me, red one for Amber. Carnation Instant Breakfast for me, bowl of cereal for Amber.) My mom had signed up as a chaperone and was jumpy all morning—I figured she was just excited, too.

I was straightening up my bed, when I heard Amber shout, "Holy crap!"

Then she said, "No way. No freakin' way!" And then she whooped, and my mom laughed out loud, and I came out to see what was going on.

There, right there in our driveway, was the biggest limousine I'd ever seen—gleaming and black, and wonderfully out of place in front of our little brick house.

"You're kidding!" I said.

My mom beamed. "I thought we should go to the airport in style."

I squealed, then threw my arms around my mom.

A *limousine*. Even the mom who always said yes, the mom who was always up for anything, could still manage to surprise me.

Moments later, the chauffeur loaded our luggage into the trunk, and we climbed into the back of the vehicle, where there were colorful lights and bottles of pop and water that we could just take, and tiny candies that we could eat. We put sunglasses on and leaned back in our seats.

"Dahling," I said, drawing out my words. "I so love traveling in style, don't you?"

"Why it's the only way to travel," said Amber, her nose high in the air.

When we rolled up to the airport, we felt like celebrities.

"Don't look around to see if anyone's watching us," said Amber. "Just look like we do this all the time."

"Right," I said.

And that's what we did. The chauffeur opened the doors for us, and we stepped out of the limousine, staring nonchalantly into the air, as if we did this sort of thing—riding in a limousine, jetting off to Florida—every other week. I felt everyone's eyes on us.

In Florida, Amber and I shared a hotel room. My mom stayed in a different room, on a different floor, with another chaperone. Amber and I could barely sleep, we were so excited. In the dark, the light coming through the crack in the curtains, we talked about the plane ride down, about how the Clarkstown kids had taken up half the plane. We talked about what it might be like tomorrow, when we sang in the park, about how this whole thing was a dream come true.

I mean, we were *here*. In Orlando, Florida. We were in our own hotel room. We were going to sing in Walt Disney World.

In the morning, we knocked on the door of my mom's hotel room. I expected that she would be as giddy as we were. But instead, her jaw was clenched tight, and her neck was splotchy, the way it became whenever she was angry. "Jeez, Mom. What's up?" I asked as we walked down the hallway.

"Nothing," she snapped.

I'm telling you, no one on this planet is worse at hiding her emotions than my mom is.

"Come on, Mom. What's going on?"

When she didn't say anything, I glanced at Amber.

"Mom?"

"I got a phone call last night, that's all," she said. "A prank." I swear, it looked like steam might start coming out of her ears, like what happens to cartoon characters when they get angry.

"What, in your hotel room?" asked Amber. My mom nodded, her nostrils flaring. Whatever it was, she was furious about it.

We entered the hotel lobby, which was packed with Clarkstown kids. My mother surveyed the crowd.

"What did they say?" I whispered.

My mom pressed her lips together, her eyes darting from face to face. God, she was really mad.

"Mrs. Rawl?" said Amber. "Was it kids?"

"Oh, yeah, it was kids all right. Boys."

Her eyes narrowed as she watched a group of boys making cups of hot chocolate. Near them, a man in a business suit tried to maneuver his way through the crowd toward the coffee machine. I felt sorry for that man. I felt sorry for anyone who was staying in the hotel who wasn't associated with Clarkstown. We were so loud.

"Mom, seriously. What did they say?"

But then Mrs. Kay was at the front of the room, waving her

hands to get everyone's attention. "The shuttles are here to take us to the park," she called out. "Please get on in an orderly fashion and remember that you are representing your school."

We began walking toward the buses.

"Mom? What did they say?"

She frowned. "They said, 'Is it true your daughter has AIDS?' And they were laughing like it was all a big goddamned joke."

"Oh, Mrs. Rawl," said Amber.

"Then they called back again. When I picked up, I said I was going to have the call traced, so they hung up. Yeah, real funny. My daughter is HIV positive, and you think it's just hilarious."

We got onto the bus and sat down.

Two rows behind us sat Michael and Kyle, who were laughing with some other boys.

My mom pressed her lips together tightly, and then said loudly—so loudly that everyone around us could hear—"If I find out who was calling the room and talking shit, there is going to be trouble."

Amber burst out laughing, but I cringed. "Mom . . ." I hissed.

"I'm sorry, but I'm *pissed*." God, her voice was so loud. "Little *jerks*." She shouted that last line into the air.

I met Amber's eyes, and she smiled at me, clearly amused by my mom. The bus rumbled into motion. The other kids started talking, but none of us spoke until we were near the park, until we could see bushes trimmed into the shape of animals.

That's when my mom looked at me. Her face had changed by now. There was less anger, more sorrow.

"Is this what it's like, Paige?" she asked. And I knew what she was thinking: if they would treat a parent this way, what must it be like for me, when parents weren't around? I could tell she was worried now.

The bus slowed down as we approached the gate. Her question hovered in the air. *Is this what it's like now?*

I shrugged. "I dunno. Sometimes. It's okay."

We sang outside, on a big outdoor stage. In front of us were many chairs in neat rows. And the funny thing was that almost nobody was in those chairs. The entire area was near empty. It turns out that when people travel to Walt Disney World, they are more interested in the rides than in hearing a bunch of middle school kids from Indiana sing.

We sang "Blue Skies" and "Pennies from Heaven" and a song about rejoicing in the brand-new day. We waved our arms and spun and wove in and out of one another as we sang. And the whole thing was a bit like the opening number of a pageant, except for the fact that we were outdoors instead of in a hotel room, and so few people were watching. My mom took pictures; I saw her out there, holding up her phone, and the sight of her alone, all of those empty chairs around her, made me so sad.

I wished that they hadn't done it, those boys.

I wished that they had left my mom alone.

It was one thing to call *me* names, to keep things kid to kid. But this was my mom, and all she ever wanted was to make me happy, and it was like they were saying to her face, *"You can't."*

My mom was right. Some line had been crossed. Everything was unhinged.

That evening, I had another seizure. I was in the hotel room, can of Coke in my hand.

I'd had a number of seizures by now. I'd had one at Target.

I'd had one in my mother's car. I'd had one at the mall, and in the hallway after school. I'd had several in the morning, just when I was supposed to get up to begin the day. My mother would find me motionless in bed, unable to move or make eye contact.

Anyway, I recognized the signs by now—that strange distancing from everything around me, the way the world faded away.

I dropped the can of Coke. I stood still.

"Paige?" Amber said. "Is it happening again, Paige?" And already her words sounded too far away, and her face, the world, was turning that funny green-gray.

I felt cold and clammy and sweaty. Then in an instant it was all gone.

I woke up on the bed, Amber and my mom by my side. My mom told me that Amber had kept my head from hitting the floor, that she'd dragged me onto my bed. (*"Oh, please, you weigh, like, nothing,"* Amber said with a wave.) Then she got my mom, and the two of them stayed with me until I came to.

My mom tried smiling at me, but I could see that sadness in her eyes, and it made me feel sick. I felt so bad that she'd paid for a limousine, that she'd spent all that money to get me here to Disney, so that we could sing for almost no one and she could get a prank phone call one night, then be called to her passed-out daughter's hotel room the next night.

I felt so bad that I couldn't be better for her, that I couldn't stop those boys, that I couldn't keep that crazed half-angry/half-sad look from entering her eyes.

On the way home from the airport, we rode in a regular car, nothing fancy. Nobody spoke. We just looked out the window at the road signs and passing semitrucks of I-465 and remembered what it had been like in the limousine on the way to the airport, how giddy we had all been.

It felt like a hundred years ago, even though it had been just a couple of days.

The last time I visited Miss Ward's office was because I was called there.

What did I do? I wondered as I walked down the hallway toward her office. *I haven't complained about the bullying since she told me to stop causing drama.*

When I knocked on Miss Ward's door, I saw Ethan sitting there, in her office.

Well, that just about blew my mind.

But when I entered, he did not look at me.

What in the world did I do?

"Paige," Miss Ward said. "It seems we have yet another problem." She gestured toward the seat next to Ethan. I sat.

"Ethan here has reported a situation."

Ethan flicked his eyes at me quickly, then looked away. I could not make out what he was thinking.

Miss Ward explained that when Ethan entered the cafeteria for lunch, a boy shouted across the lunchroom at him.

"You'd better not kiss Paige," the boy had warned. "Or you'll get AIDS, too."

Then other kids had laughed. *"Ethan's gonna get AIDS. . . ."*

And then a few said things like, *"I'll bet he got AIDS already."*

I felt my face flush red as Miss Ward spoke. Ethan looked down at the floor. He did not say a word. When Miss Ward finished, we all sat in silence for a few awkward moments. She folded her arms.

Oh, God, I thought. *This is the worst thing ever.*

"Ethan decided to report the situation." Then she looked

at me. "Paige, I've already called the other boy's parents and discussed it with them. I'm afraid I need to call your mother, too."

Okay, wait. Here was a situation that happened when I wasn't even around. It happened to someone other than me and was started by someone other than me. When it happened, I was half a school away. Yet for some reason, she needed to call me down here to tell me about it. She needed to call my mom.

There was nothing to do but sit and wait, so that is what I did.

She dismissed Ethan, who did not look at me, did not say good-bye, when he left her office. Miss Ward dialed my mother, her long nails tap-tapping the buttons on the phone. She described the situation to my mother.

"Mmm-hmm. Yes. Yes, I'm going to send her back to class now. Okay, yes, I'll make sure Miss Fischer gets the message. Okay, Mrs. Rawl. Okay. Good-bye now."

She placed the receiver on the telephone and she looked at me.

"You may go."

I stood up.

"I really do not know what to say about any of this, Paige."

I nodded and left the room.

That afternoon, just before cheerleading, I saw Ethan waiting outside the gym.

"Hey," I said. I slowed down.

"Hey," he said. His cheeks were bright red.

I liked him so much, I could have kissed him right then and there.

And although the whole situation was mortifying, I had to admit that I liked that he told Miss Ward, liked that he defended my honor like that.

I had a thought then: *I want to show everybody.* I wanted to show everybody that I was just as deserving of love as anybody else. I wanted to show everyone that no matter what people said, this boy chose me, chose me above the rest of them.

I wanted to walk through the cafeteria with him at lunchtime holding hands. I wanted everyone to see. It was a silly thought—it seems ridiculous in retrospect—but it's what I wanted above all. I wanted it so badly I might have even slipped a note into my shoe, just like I did before winning the Indiana Sweetheart pageant.

Ethan and Paige will hold hands in front of the whole school.

He looked down at the ground. "Sorry about today."

I was about to tell him that he didn't need to apologize, that he was just reporting what someone else said. I was about to say, *Forget it*, which is what I really hoped he would do. *Forget it, let's move on, let's be boyfriend and girlfriend just like we both want.* But that was when he said to me, more quietly, "Let's not tell people we're hanging out anymore."

I stopped walking. He added quickly, "We can still hang out, of course. We just don't have to let anyone know."

I looked away, over his shoulder, into the gymnasium, where the basketball team was already starting to warm up.

"Okay," I said, like it didn't matter to me at all. "Yeah, sure. That's fine."

Red

Here is a blade, and here is my skin.

It was almost funny—although I suppose it probably was not funny at all, not in the least—the way it reminded me of that old game I once played with my hands:

Here is the church, and here is the steeple.

Here is the blade, and here is my skin.

Open it up and see all the people.

Open it up, let the bleeding begin.

This is how it happened the first time. It really was that simple. One day, I cut myself until I bled.

I was in the bathroom, music blasting. My mom had long stopped banging on the door when I did this. She just left me alone until I was ready to come out. Then she hovered in my bedroom doorway chattering about nothing at all, flashing worried glances every time I moved.

But as long as I was in the bathroom, she left me alone. She was leaving me alone right now.

The music was loud, and my skin was pale, and my blood was red. And I wasn't sure—I'm still not sure—if I was trying to hurt myself, exactly. It's more like I was trying to feel something. Like I was numb, somehow, and I didn't know any other way to make myself feel. Or maybe, instead, it was the opposite. Maybe the sharp blade was a distraction from what I felt all the time and had begun to take as normal.

My new normal. A normal where nothing was normal.

It's kind of like when you can't tell the difference between hot and cold; the two sensations—hot, cold, feeling, numb— start to seem exactly the same after a while.

But you can tell the difference between red blood and pale skin.

Here is the blade, and here is my skin.

I scraped just enough to get the top layers of skin off—not so deep that I wouldn't be able to stop the bleeding. But it worked and my blood was red, and I felt something different from what I'd been feeling.

In the end, it didn't really matter to me if that was *something* or *nothing*. Either way, it was a relief.

I felt calm.

I turned the music off and sat there, looking at my blood, listening to the sound of my own breath. (How funny, how rarely we notice that, how rarely we take the time to notice our own constant effort to stay alive.)

I pressed toilet paper down on my wrists until they stopped bleeding. Then I flushed the toilet paper, pulled the sleeves down on my sweatshirt, and went into my bedroom. My mother appeared in the doorway, and I gripped my sleeves, holding them over my wrists as she hovered. I gripped them until she was gone, until it was time to turn out the light and stare at the ceiling, waiting for sleep to come.

Withdrawal

Autumn. Eighth grade.

I was on the bench at an away soccer match.

My seizures had continued into the summer. I didn't want to pass out in front of the whole school ever again, so I didn't cheer. Instead, I tried out for the soccer team and made it. Yasmine was on the team, and I'm not sure what to say about that. Maybe I was refusing to let her get in my way—maybe I wanted to prove to her that I could go anywhere, do anything, and that she couldn't stop me. Or perhaps, instead, some part of me wanted to bring things to a head. At any rate, when I showed up at practice on the first day, her eyes flashed surprise, and I jutted out my chin and did not look at her.

We had fewer classes together this year. For one thing, Mrs. Yates had held me back in math. There would be no studying math at the high school, which maybe was just as well. Middle school kids were scary enough.

At practice, Yasmine and I passed each other the ball when we had to. Otherwise, she and I had become like the magnets that a teacher once showed us in science class, the kind that don't ever touch, no matter how much you try to push them together.

But I liked soccer, liked most of the girls on the team. Besides, I liked the coach, Miss Ryan. She was sporty and young and blond, energetic and pretty. She was *cool*, kids said. *Miss Ryan is cool.*

This match was early in the season. I sat next to Miss Ryan, waiting to be put into the game. Yasmine was in midfield, dashing toward an opposing player who dribbled the ball. Yasmine charged the girl—I swear, she was afraid of nothing. Everyone knew what would happen next. Even members of the opposing team saw it coming. One swipe of the foot, and the ball was Yasmine's, just like that.

The parents behind us cheered. I watched, but remained silent.

Miss Ryan turned to me then.

"By the way, Paige," Miss Ryan said. She said it casually. Too casually, actually. It was as if we weren't in the middle of a game at the moment, as if we had all the time in the world for conversation.

The back of my neck felt prickly, and I sat up a little straighter.

"I heard"—oh my God, the laid-back voice of hers—"that you had AIDS. Is that true?"

I glanced at her. Miss Ryan's eyes surveyed the field as if she hadn't said anything at all.

We were mere inches from other kids, just a few feet from the parents behind us on the bleachers. An opposing player kicked the ball out-of-bounds. The ref blew his whistle, and the girls gathered for the throw-in.

It's funny how you think about the right responses only in retrospect. I mean, now I can think of plenty of things I might have said. And I wish I'd said any of them. I wish I'd told her that HIV and AIDS are not the same thing, and that anybody who knows anything knows that. I wish I'd thought to say that it's against the law to disclose someone's health without their permission, so perhaps she should keep her voice a little lower.

Most of all, I wish I had said four simple words: "None of your business."

But sitting there on the metal bench, blue-and-white jerseys moving all around me on a green field, I was just a kid. I was a kid who was different from all those other kids in shin guards and cleats, different from all those parents who might be listening. I was a kid who was sitting next to a teacher that everyone universally agreed was cool, and I wanted her to like me.

So I said just one word: "No."

And while that was technically true—I didn't have AIDS, and as long as I could keep my CD4 cells above two hundred, I wouldn't have it—I didn't say it to be accurate. I said it because it was all I could think to say, the only way I knew to make the conversation stop.

"Huh," said Miss Ryan, as if we were talking about the weather. Like, *Huh, it really is a lovely fall afternoon.*

Huh, the trees are starting to change color, have you noticed?

Huh, might start to get colder next week.

Huh, I think you are lying to me and that you really have AIDS.

One of our players kicked the ball hard, and both teams rushed toward the opposing goal.

And then, just like that—so quickly I almost questioned whether the moment had happened—she put me back in the game. I ran past Yasmine on my way in, and we did not look at each other.

Later, when I told my mother what Miss Ryan asked, she was furious. A few days later, during team photographs, she confronted Miss Ryan.

"What are you doing, asking her if she's got AIDS?" my mom demanded. Although she had pulled Miss Ryan aside, her voice was louder than usual. Miss Ryan glanced around, embarrassed. She told my mother that she had just wanted to dispel a rumor, that another child had told her I had AIDS. She thought she was merely putting a rumor to rest.

"Can you imagine what that felt like for her, to have her coach ask her in the middle of a game?"

Shhhh, I wanted to say to my mother. *Everybody can hear you.*

"Well, I looked in her medical file," said Miss Ryan. "But I didn't see any record of it."

My mom's face turned beet red. "Excuse me?"

"I just . . ." Miss Ryan started.

"You checked her confidential file?"

"Mrs. Rawl, I—"

Then my mother said what I hadn't thought to say. "It's none of your damn business!" By the end of the sentence her voice had risen to almost a shriek.

It is possible to be both mortified and satisfied at the same time. I know this, because I felt both things, in equal measure, when I looked at Miss Ryan's stunned face.

Miss Ryan's voice was lower than my mom's, but I could still hear her. "Don't you think that as her coach, I am entitled to know?"

"Entitled to know?" screeched my mom. "Entitled to know? You're not 'entitled' to know anything!"

Miss Ryan frowned. "Why don't we both calm down, Mrs. Rawl?"

"We? You mean me. You're telling *me* to calm down. But I'm not *going* to calm down," my mother said, "because I know the law. The law says that HIV status is confidential. Completely confidential."

"Come on, Mrs. Rawl. I'm her coach."

"Yeah, and how do I know you don't have HIV?"

Miss Ryan took a deep breath, then looked right in my mother's eyes. "Mrs. Rawl, what if something happened? What if she started bleeding on the field?"

"What if any kid started bleeding on the field!" my mom

shouted. "You avoid all blood, everyone's blood, because you never know who's got what!"

Miss Ryan stared off in the distance for a moment, then turned to my mom.

"Actually," said Miss Ryan, her teeth flashing. She burst out with a small laugh, a false laugh, the kind of laugh that has nothing to do with anything around it. "We can use Paige's HIV to our advantage. The players on the other team will be afraid to touch her. She will be able to score all the goals."

Later, Miss Ryan would deny having said this. Under oath, literally swearing to God, she would deny it. And who knows—maybe she truly didn't remember that part of the conversation. But I'm telling you: I was standing right there, and I heard it. I heard those words clear as day.

I remember them all these years later, just as I remember the wave of shame that came over me when I heard them.

Words like that, the kind that make you feel low and filthy and ashamed, you never forget.

I'd always loved playing soccer, but when my coach said the team could use my HIV status to score more goals, it was one of the lowest points of my time in middle school.

. . .

That night, I dumped out my backpack in the middle of the living-room floor—just shook it until there was nothing left inside. Then I picked up my notebooks and tore them, one by one. I ripped the pages out of my books, crumpled them and threw them on the floor.

"What are you doing?" my mom asked.

I tore. Crumpled.

"Paige," she said sharply.

I made a noise, a cross between a scream and a growl. It sounded feral, and it scared me a little.

It certainly seemed to scare my mother. Her face contorted into a look I'd never seen before. "Paige," she said more carefully. "Come on, you're going to need those."

I grabbed chunks of paper from my math notebook, as many as I could tear out in a single chunk, and I threw the pieces on the floor.

"Paige," my mother started to plead. "Come on. That's your schoolwork. You can't do that."

I didn't answer her. I just took another chunk of paper, then another, until I held nothing but two covers, dangling from a pulled-out metal spiral. I threw that against the front door, and turned to my social studies book.

My mom was crying by now. "Stop," she said. "Come on, just stop it, Paige!"

But I didn't stop. I tore it all, workbooks, notebooks—all the careful notes I'd been taking in classes. Photocopied work sheets, one after another. Vocabulary words. Lab reports.

All that work. All of that optimism. It all lay in a giant heap on the floor.

No matter what I did, I was always going to be seen as the kid causing problems. I was the bad kid. It didn't matter that

I hadn't done anything wrong, that my HIV, the source of all the trouble, just came out with me on my first day in this world, the way other kids emerged with blond hair or freckles.

But HIV wasn't like freckles. It wasn't freckles or curly hair or green eyes or dark skin. It wasn't anything like those things.

HIV made me bad, somehow. Less deserving.

Those other kids would never get in trouble. I was the problem. It would always be me.

I kicked my papers and books then. I kicked until my feet hurt, kicked until I was exhausted. Then I dropped to the floor and sobbed.

I never wanted to go back to school there. Not ever. Even my mother couldn't make me go. Not tomorrow, not next week, not ever.

On September 23, Dr. Cox and my mother sat down with Miss Fischer for a meeting. There were others there, too: the director of the school district and the head of athletics. My mom had told Dr. Cox that she planned to withdraw me from Clarkstown, that she wanted to homeschool me. Dr. Cox thought it was important that everybody sit in the room together at least once, before we made the final decision.

At that meeting, Miss Fischer told my mom that she hadn't known I had HIV.

(*Really?* I would wonder later when I heard this. Miss Ward never told her? Besides, Miss Fischer was always in the cafeteria, in the hallways, at games. She never heard anyone call me "PAIDS"?)

She told my mom that no one in the administrative office knew what had been written in the notes I'd received.

She told my mom that they did not keep records from the school counselors' office.

(*Seriously?* I would wonder. The counselors' office doesn't document *anything*? The counselors are just supposed to somehow kind of remember what happens to nine hundred children?)

She told my mom that she would create a sensitivity plan and send it to Dr. Cox.

(None of us ever saw it.)

As the meeting came to a close, Dr. Cox said that in her professional judgment, my mom was probably right: that based on what she'd learned, she didn't think the environment was conducive to my well-being. That it made sense to opt for homeschooling.

She looked forward to seeing Miss Fischer's sensitivity plan.

My mom filed the papers the next day. I went with her and, as she stood in the office, I walked into my classrooms, placed my textbooks on the teachers' desks, then walked out again. I felt my fellow students' eyes on me.

I did not know if I was doing something brave or cowardly.

I saw Miss Fischer only briefly that day. She spoke to me slowly, the way you would speak to a very young child.

"I wish you could continue to attend Clarkstown," said Miss Fischer. "But I cannot promise to protect you."

I imagined her finishing that sentence. Although she didn't say these words, here is what I heard:

After all, there is only so much a girl with HIV can expect.

I shrugged and did not look at her.

I walked outside. It was a dazzling autumn day, the sun beaming down from clear blue sky. On one field, there was a football game, on another, a soccer game. If things had been different, I would have been out there, too, still cheering with those kids in skirts who jumped and kicked.

A seventh-grade student, a girl named Erin who had just come to Clarkstown this year, rushed over to me. "Paige," she cried out. "Is it true? Are you actually leaving?"

"Yeah," I said. I nodded. "I am."

"Lucky," she laughed. Then she quickly added, "I'm just kidding. I don't mean that you're lucky for—"

"I know."

"I'm just sad," she said quietly. "That's all."

Behind us, a referee blew a whistle. The crowd in the bleachers cheered. I felt the sun on my arms; it felt warm and lovely, totally out of sync with everything I'd been feeling for so long.

"Hey, can we take a picture together?" Erin asked, perking up a little.

I nodded "Sure."

I still have that photo. We are squinting slightly from the sun. I am wearing a red T-shirt. Erin's arm, the one that holds the camera, is extended, and we are both looking up. Our faces are pressed together, and it almost looks like one of her eyebrows is running into mine.

We look happy in that moment. Both of us do.

My mom walked out of the buildings with a stack of papers. She looked tired—more tired than I'd seen her look in a long, long time.

"Paige." She waved to me.

"I gotta go," I said to Erin.

"Okay," said Erin, then she gave me a hug. When her arms were wrapped around me, she whispered, "Keep in touch."

"I will."

She pulled back and looked directly at me, her mouth twisted into a half smile, half frown.

She was sad, I realized. This girl was genuinely sad I was leaving.

"Promise?" she asked.

I nodded and I smiled at her. "Yeah, Erin, I do." I meant it, too. "I promise."

I ran to catch up with my mom. We got into the car and pulled out of the lot.

I never returned to Clarkstown Middle School.

I Just Want to Do Something

Not long after I left Clarkstown, I sat on the sofa glumly flipping through channels on the television. A news show. An entertainment show. Some reality show where people eat gross things and try not to gag. I wasn't interested in any of it.

"You want something to eat?" my mom offered. I shook my head.

She stood in the doorway for a while, watching me. Then she said, "You know what? I want you to watch something else."

"I'm okay." I clicked the remote. A game show. An old sitcom. Some lawyer drama.

"No, Paige. I want you to see something." She disappeared for a moment; when she returned, she held a video. She handed it to me: *The Ryan White Story*. It looked old and grainy, like it was filmed in some long-ago decade.

Ugh, I thought. *One of my mom's stupid old movies.*

"Do I have to?"

She didn't answer me. Instead, she turned off my channel, popped the movie in, and settled down on the sofa next to me.

It was weird, because I recognized everything I saw in the opening credits. There was the Indiana War Memorial, one of the major monuments of downtown. There was the larger-than-life Marilyn Monroe cutout from a bar on Jackson Street, and the Indianapolis Motor Speedway. There, on the screen in front of me, were things I recognized from my own life: guys in Indiana University and Colts jerseys, cans of beer in their hands. JESUS SAVES mission signs and CASH FOR GOLD signs. I saw cornfields and silos, KIWANIS CLUB signs and LIONS CLUB signs, the long, flat roads of Indiana, looming water towers.

I realized I'd never watched a movie that had been filmed in my own state. I leaned my head against my mom and snuggled my body closer to her.

I watched. I watched as a skinny kid named Ryan—a kid with a paper route, a kid who was in middle school, a nice kid, the kind I would have liked—coughed uncomfortably. We watched as a doctor click-clicked his ball-point pen just before telling Ryan's mom her son had AIDS.

"Is this real?" I asked.

"Yes," she whispered.

"It's a true story?"

"Completely true," she said, her eyes still on the screen. "He was about my age."

My mother pulled a cheetah-patterned fleece blanket over our laps.

In the movie, Ryan's school district expelled him, just for his having been infected. I turned to my mother.

"That's not fair," I said.

She hit pause with the remote control.

"It's not, Paige," she said. Even then, she explained, doctors had been clear: there was no way Ryan's classmates could have possibly contracted the disease from him at school. Mom repeated what I'd known for a long time—what everyone knew by now, even if they chose to ignore it: the illness cannot be spread by touch, by drinking fountains, by toilets, or by anything else that could have possibly happened within the walls of middle school.

"Just like," she finished, "there's no reason for your classmates to feel like you're any different. If they knew it even back in Ryan's time, there's no excuse for not knowing it now."

Ryan's mother filed a lawsuit. She wanted him to attend school. Then other parents in the district responded by filing their own suit. They wanted him to stay home. People screamed that he should be quarantined until he died. Although a judge ruled that he could attend school, nearly half the students stayed home. Students moved their desks away from him; they steered clear of him in the hallway. People scrawled hateful messages across his books and on his locker.

Someone shot a gun into the family's living room.

I watched, then, as Ryan's mother tried to explain the ugliest part of humanity to her child.

And I knew then, that this, right here, was my mom's own way of explaining things. This movie, ordering it and watching it with me, was her way of trying to explain what had happened to me. This was her way of showing me, as best as she knew how, that it wasn't my fault, that what had happened to me at school wasn't something I'd deserved.

In a funny way, I realized, what had happened to me wasn't even about me. It was something about people. Something that was wrong with people.

It hadn't just happened to me, either. There had been this boy. There were surely others out there right this very moment.

That fact, that there were others, made me feel better and worse at the same time.

When the movie was over, I turned to my mom and asked her, "Mom, why do people . . . ?" My voice trailed off. I think what I wanted to say was, *Why do they choose hate?* I couldn't quite find the words, though. I shook my head, frustrated.

She seemed to understand. "I don't know, Paige. They're ignorant, that's all." That may have been the true answer, the right one—but it wasn't good enough for me.

"So . . ." I was mad suddenly. I was really, really angry. "So that's it? We just accept that? People are ignorant and that's that?"

She placed the blanket back over us, but I pushed it away.

She sighed. "I'm upset, too, Paige. I hate this."

"But it's not right," I said. I realized how young I sounded, how close I was to whining. I couldn't stop myself. "It's not *fair.*"

My mom reached out to pull me close, but I leaned far away from her. I didn't want her hugs, didn't want her sympathy. I wanted things to be different—really, really different.

"Paige, I just—"

"No," I insisted. "It's not fair. It's not fair that all of those other kids still get to go to school."

I began to cry, really cry.

"They did this," I continued. "They're the ones who did the wrong thing." I wasn't even sure my words were coming out clearly, I was crying so hard. "*They* should have to withdraw, not me."

Tomorrow, all my classmates would be at Clarkstown, just like every other day. They'd be in classes, looking through microscopes, running around the track, cracking jokes in the hallway. They would be together, passing notes and cramming for the geometry quiz and shooting straw wrappers at each other at lunchtime. Their world would go on like it always had. The only thing missing would be me.

I'd be here. I'd be all alone.

I would have just disappeared, which is what some of them

probably wanted all along.

I sobbed and sobbed, my back heaving as I gasped for breath.

"Oh, Paige," my mom said. "Oh, my sweet Paige."

I cried into the darkness of the sofa. My mom rubbed my back, back and forth, back and forth, as I gasped and shook, and curled into a tiny ball.

Eventually, I must have fallen asleep, because when I opened my eyes again, it was dark outside. There was a blanket over me, and I could smell fried chicken. I walked into the kitchen and saw my mother's backside; her head was stuffed in the refrigerator, and I could hear jars rattling around. I stood there until she closed the door, looked up at me, surprised. "Hey, sweetie," she said. "You hungry? I was just saving some dinner for you."

The light above the oven was on. I could see tiny droplets of grease glistening on the stovetop. Mom picked up a sponge and started wiping everything down.

My mother, always trying to clean up a mess.

I didn't feel sad anymore. I didn't feel angry. It turns out a person can cry those things right out of their system, drain themselves of all that.

What's left behind, after all of that goes, is a kind of determination.

"Honey?" she asked. "You okay?"

When I spoke, my voice was level—so flat I barely recognized it as my own.

"I just want to do something," I said. "That's all."

On November 18, my mother and I filed a lawsuit in the US Federal District Court, Southern Indiana District. The suit alleged that the school had failed to protect me from bullying, and that this failure was against the law—against two laws, in fact.

Lawsuits have lots of fancy terms—"mumbo jumbo," my mom called it after we sat in the lawyer's office for the first time. But the facts turned out to be pretty simple. Long before I was born, two laws—the Americans with Disabilities Act and the Rehabilitation Act of 1973—established that no one with a disability, or even a perceived disability, could be denied fair treatment under the law. "Fair treatment" included the ability to go to school without being harassed.

In other words, kids who are disabled—or even perceived in some way to be disabled—have a right to free public education without harassment.

"But am I disabled?" I asked my mom later as she tried to explain it to me.

She told me that she never thought of me as disabled, and she was proud that I never considered myself disabled. But the law was clear on this: HIV and AIDS are classified as disabilities.

"So if you were harassed in a way that interfered with your education," my mom continued, "and the school didn't change things, it meant the school broke the law."

She explained that our case boiled down to three questions:

First, was I ever bullied?

Second, did the school know about it?

Third, if so, had the school taken reasonable steps to stop the bullying, to create a safe environment for me?

If we could establish that they hadn't—if they hadn't done enough—then we would win.

It's a funny thing, filing a lawsuit. Everyone who files a lawsuit says they don't care about the money. They all say that, again and again, using the same words every time: *It's not about the money.* I know how suspicious that sounds. A lawsuit, after all, is all about money; if you win, you get money. Money is the end point, the reward for being right.

And while that may be the case, I can also tell you that money is just a stand-in for something bigger, something more important.

I walked away from Clarkstown needing something I hadn't gotten. I needed someone to tell me that what happened to me wasn't okay. That it was wrong for kids to call me "PAIDS," wrong for them to make me feel ashamed of who I was, wrong for a coach to single me out, to look at my health records and make a joke about my infection. I needed someone to validate that: that the whole thing—the notes, the comments, the nickname, the whispers, the gossip, the fact that all my complaints were dismissed or labeled as drama—was just plain wrong. That there was nothing so wrong with me that I deserved to be humiliated.

I wanted someone to tell me that I was okay.

And I will admit, too, that I also wanted something else, something a little less noble: I wanted to see them squirm. All of them: the boys who called me PAIDS, and all the kids who laughed when they heard it. Miss Fischer and Miss Ryan and Miss Ward. Everyone who had made me feel so awful for so long. I wanted to see them take the stand, face the lawyer's questions, look me in the eye.

I wanted them to feel what I had, to know exactly what it was that I had experienced.

Those were the things I was after: First, a recognition that I wasn't really to blame for all that had happened. Second, I wanted people to know exactly what it was like to feel on the defensive. And while I didn't exactly want a lawsuit, neither my mom nor I could figure out any better way get the things I really did want.

"We'll win, won't we, Mom?" I asked.

"Well." She paused. "Let me ask you this. Did those kids hurt you?"

I nodded.

"Did they hurt you so much you found it hard to learn?"

I thought about my missed assignments, all those times I couldn't concentrate, the seizures. "Uh-huh."

"You remember all those times I called the office and nobody ever called me back?"

"Yeah."

"The notes I left?"

"Yeah. I remember."

"So do *you* think the school took reasonable steps?"

I shook my head. As far as I could tell, aside from that time my mom and Yasmine's dad had been called into the office, and the time the boy had made fun of Ethan in the cafeteria, no one had ever gotten in trouble.

She sighed and wrapped her arm around me tight. "So, we'll win," she said. "Open-and-shut case."

Then she leaned back and held up her hand, an invitation to a high five. I slapped her hand with my own.

On the Tuesday before Thanksgiving, just a few days after we filed the suit, the phone rang. I was in my bedroom, trying to focus on reading. It was hard to concentrate on my work—the days at home just seemed to run into one another.

I heard my mother answer, then I heard alarm in her voice. I walked out into the kitchen.

"Okay," she said. "Okay, uh-huh. Yeah. Okay, Oh, jeez. Oh, God. Okay."

She hung up the phone and turned to me.

"Oh, God, Paige."

"What is it?"

"That was our lawyer."

"What did he say?"

My mom's face was pale. She didn't say anything. The refrigerator hummed. Outside the window, a car passed by, music blasting; I could hear the *thud-thud-thud* of the beat get louder, then fade quickly away.

"Mom?"

"He just got off the phone with someone at the *Indianapolis Star*."

My stomach lurched. "Why?"

"They wanted a comment," she said. "About the lawsuit."

I let that news sink in.

"It's going to be in the newspaper?"

My mom was still standing there, phone in her hand. She nodded. "I guess so."

I shook my head. "That can't be right. It's supposed to be confidential. I thought that because I'm just a kid, it was supposed to be confidential."

My mom shook her head. "I don't know," she said. "But it's out. Oh, God, Paige, now everyone is going to know." Her face was panicked.

I sat down and thought about this. It almost struck me as funny: I had told just one person about my HIV—my best friend, then a sixth grader. Soon, the whole school knew. And now, all of Indianapolis was about to know, as well.

I wondered if Yasmine could have ever guessed her own power. I thought about her at age eleven, and wondered if she could possibly have ever imagined that she was capable of setting into place a chain reaction, one that would affect what a city of close to a million people would know about one of its residents.

I remembered that very first glimpse I had of her—how

she'd struck me as strong and intense, the unusual confidence she seemed to radiate as she hushed those kids laughing in the auditorium. I could never have guessed. I could never have guessed then how everything would unfold. And yet now, as I waited for the news of my HIV to explode like a bomb across my hometown, the whole thing struck me as almost inevitable, like it had been preordained from that first sighting.

Mom stood up. "I'm going to call Heather's family," she said. "I don't want them to find out about all of this by reading it in the paper."

"The lawsuit?"

"All of it. The lawsuit, the fact that you have HIV."

"You do, too, you know."

"Yes, Paige. That, too. They've been good to us. They should hear it from us."

She picked up her phone and dialed. I walked into my room, shaking a little.

"Hi, it's Sandy," I could hear my mother saying. "Yeah. Mmm-hmm. Yeah, everything's good. I just wanted to—well, there's going to be something in the paper tomorrow, and I just wanted to tell you about it."

I closed the door to my room.

A little while later, my mom knocked. "Paige," she said. "Heather is on the phone for you."

I took the phone. "Hello?"

"Paige," said Heather. Her voice was completely calm. "You know what? You're the very best. And I love you."

The story appeared online late that night; my mom and I read it out loud to each other a few different times. I listened to my own experiences discussed in the third person, and it felt like I was having an out-of-body experience, like on some level the story had ceased to be about me at all.

By morning, the print version of the *Star* hit doorsteps all over the city. I was right there on the front page. We were front page news—"front Paige news," my mom and I joked, laughing louder than we should have about the pun.

I imagined Clarkstown families reading the stories—Michael Jepson's parents, for example. Or Devin Holt's. Or the kid who told Ethan not to kiss me. I knew none of the parents would ever connect the story they were reading to their own child; they would never stop to wonder if their own sons and daughters were among the name-callers. They would assume it was other kids. I felt sure of that.

Everyone, I knew by now, always assumed it was someone else's kid.

On television, news reporters were interviewing my classmates and their parents. In the television shot, we could see a news van parked in front of the school, exactly where I'd walked so many times. My mom and I spent the morning peeking out from behind our curtains, wondering if a news van would descend upon our house the way they had on Ryan White's. They never came.

"Well, that's a relief," my mom said.

"So maybe things are getting better for people with HIV?" I suggested.

My mom settled into our sofa and sighed. "I hope so, pumpkin."

Within a day, the story had been picked up by national papers: the *Boston Globe*, the *Huffington Post*, MSNBC, even the Centers for Disease Control and Prevention. *That's me they're talking about*, I would think as I saw the headlines. *They're talking about me in Boston. In Washington, DC.*

Some of the stories had comments attached, most of them expressing outrage at how I'd been treated.

> *Goddamnit. This is something the teachers should know could happen, and should run interference on. I'm a teacher— this is one of the terrible possibilities we must always be on the alert for. . . . Those students in that middle school need to be shown the consequences of expressing such hatred.*

Strangers, at least, were rooting for me, rooting for a world that was a little kinder than it was.

A thought began to form in my mind, a feeling that I couldn't quite articulate. It had to do with how large the world seemed, and how small, all at once, and what my role in it might be. I couldn't quite put it into words at the time; I just knew it made me feel restless, like there was something important I needed to be doing.

It was only later, much later, that I would begin to recognize those moments for what they were: a dawning awareness of my own influence, the idea that I could make a difference.

PART THREE

Falling

Community

I heard the thudding bass drumbeat before I heard the rest of the band. Already I could see red balloons, red T-shirts, red shorts, all varieties of red streaming toward the downtown War Museum.

We were headed to the Indiana AIDS Walk—me, my mom, Erin, and Amber.

The woman who coordinated my medical care had encouraged me to come.

"It's a three-mile walk," she had explained at one of my appointments. "It raises money for AIDS services and research. But it's so much more than that."

"How do you mean?" I asked.

She smiled. "You'll understand when you see it."

She leaned in to me then. "Paige," she said, looking me right in the eye. "I really do think you should see it."

I'd been lonely. Since leaving Clarkstown, I'd been sitting inside. I did my schoolwork quietly at the dining room table, all the while imagining what was happening back at school.

Now they are in social studies, I would think.

Now they are in gym class.

The clock ticked. Cars passed on the street outside my house. On the radio, Taylor Swift's voice gave way to Kid Rock.

Now everyone is getting ready for cheerleading practice. Now choir.

Then I would finish my homework and wonder, *Now what?*

Ethan still texted me from time to time, which made me feel happy and sad, all at once. Erin and Mariah and Amber called me, too; I'd talk to them on the phone about *American Idol,* about the latest Nickelback song. I'd laugh with Mariah about her overweight cat, Fat Louie. But we rarely talked much about school. A few others checked in from time to time, but it was hard to know what to talk to them about.

They were in one place. I was in another place entirely.

In the place where I was, emptiness could squeeze the breath right out of you. In the place where I was, every day was a steady, dank gray drizzle.

Which was why, walking toward the AIDS Walk now, I had to struggle to make sense of it all—the clear deep blue above our heads, the unseasonably warm air, the bands playing in the distance, the festive mood that seemed to surround us.

Until this moment, having HIV had brought me nothing but isolation, nothing but sadness. It had made me feel alone, without any sort of community to call my own.

So who were all of these people? And why did they seem so upbeat?

Walking toward the registration desk, I paused for a moment. I wasn't sure I had it in me to take another step toward that noisy, cheerful crowd.

My mom put her hand gently on my back. "Come on, pumpkin," she said.

I took a deep breath.

In front of me, Amber and Erin stood waiting. Amber caught my eye and grinned. She began shaking her hips in time with the drumbeat. Then Erin did the same.

A man and a woman dressed all in red walked past me with two small children. The kids, one small boy and one small girl, wore rainbow tutus. They bounced as they walked. They were happy.

Watching those kids, watching my friends dancing in front of me, I thought I could almost remember what happy felt like.

I took a deep breath.

Okay, I thought. *Let's do this.*

Amber, Erin, and me at the Indiana AIDS Walk in 2008.
We were so surprised at how fun the day was, and having
my friends with me gave me courage to meet new people.

As my mom turned in our registration forms, Erin and Amber and I strolled past the information booths that had been set up by service organizations. Every one handed out gifts of some kind. One had a bowl of shiny red Mardi Gras beads. I stuck my hand into the bowl, feeling the beads on my fingers.

"Ooh," said Erin. "I want some."

A man behind the booth said, "Take some." I took one for each of us. The man said. "Aw, you can take more than that." He grabbed a handful for us, and we draped them around our necks. In other booths we snagged different gifts, too: temporary tattoos in the shape of red ribbons, rainbow stickers, red plastic sunglasses, and little red tote bags. We picked up keychains and stress balls, pencils and pens, and refrigerator magnets. We stopped in front of a booth with Hershey's Kisses wrapped in red foil. They were already melty from the eighty-degree heat, but I didn't care—I unwrapped a couple of them and popped them in my mouth at the same time.

"That's what I'm talking about," Erin said, taking a couple for herself.

Amber picked up the bowl and pretended she was going to sneak off with the whole thing. Then, a few steps away from the booth, turned around. "All right, all right," she said to no one in particular. "I won't take more than my share. . . ." She unwrapped a single Hershey's Kiss and popped it in her mouth, grinning.

Someone handed me a fact sheet, and I scanned, my mouth still filled with chocolate: nearly ten thousand residents of Indiana infected with HIV or AIDS. Every county affected. Nationally, more than a million people infected. And every month, nearly a thousand teens and young people newly affected in the United States alone.

Whoa. Did I read that right? I re-read it, and there it was in black and white: Every month. Nearly a thousand teens newly infected.

That's when I had this thought: *Someone should really talk about that.*

We stepped up to the booth of an organization called Women in Motion. A lady in a red T-shirt and baseball cap greeted us.

"What brings you girls to the walk?" she asked, smiling at me warmly.

I hesitated for a moment. Already I'd learned a hard lesson about what happens when you tell someone about having

HIV. But still: if there was any place on earth where I could tell someone without being rejected, it was probably here.

So I told her. Just like that, I said it: "I have HIV."

She didn't widen her eyes, or show any kind of shock. She just looked me in the eye and nodded knowingly. "How are you doing?" she asked.

Her voice was so genuine, so kind, it felt like my heart cracked open. My words came tumbling out. I told her my whole story—what a terrible time I'd had at school. How I had chosen homeschooling over the notes and name-calling. How I was fine physically, I guessed, but was just kind of—well, *really very*—alone.

"They all get to go on with their lives like nothing happened. And I'm in solitary confinement," I finished. Then I shook my head. "The whole thing stinks."

The woman, whose name—I could see her name tag now—was Marie, placed her hand, ever so gently, on mine. "You know, we do many events and we are always looking for speakers. Would you ever consider telling your story at one?"

"Well . . . maybe . . ." I said.

I must not have sounded terribly convincing, because she grinned at me. "Just do me a favor," she said. "Think about it."

"Okay," I told her. "I'll think about it." I dropped her business card in my bag.

That's when my mom appeared. "Girls, come with me. I want you to see something."

I could still feel Marie's touch on my hand as my mom led us toward the steps of the War Memorial. There, large swatches of fabric were draped over the stairs.

The AIDS Quilt. A memorial to people who died of AIDS.

"What is this?" Erin asked.

My mom tried to explain. "Before you guys were born, there had been so much stigma, so much shame about HIV/AIDS, that sometimes people's family members wouldn't acknowledge their deaths. Other times, funeral homes refused to handle the person's body out of fear that they might catch the disease. There was no way to properly remember the victims. So friends and loved ones found a different way to honor them. They started sewing quilt panels—one for each person who lost their life to the disease. The AIDS Quilt is now the largest community folk art project in human history. This is just one small piece of it."

So each piece, every one, was a memory of someone gone.

I tried to take in every single panel. One featured about a hundred mallard ducks. I wondered if the person it represented had been a hunter. Another was made from sports shirts—Pacers, Colts, the Indianapolis Ice, WrestleMania. Yet another showed a man in a top hat dancing on piano keys. The most somber panel had just five letters—*BRUCE*—appliquéd over a black background.

But they weren't just sad. They were colorful, too. Many of them featured rainbows. A shooting star leaving a rainbow trail. A sailboat with rainbow flags billowing behind it. A kite tethered to rainbow ribbons. A can of paint spilled into a rainbow road, with the words *Peter, Peter Painter Man. See you on the flip side.*

I squinted at the quilt panels and tried to imagine the people—the real individuals whom each panel honored. I imagined that each was seated on the steps of the memorial, and each of them was smiling. No longer in pain. No longer sick. No longer hated or scorned or feared.

I closed my eyes and whispered a silent prayer for them.

I wished them peace.

When I opened my eyes again, only cloth remained.

My mother put her arm around me, and we stood there for a moment together. Neither of us said it out loud, but I knew we were both thinking about my dad.

A fresh round of marching music drifted to us from the bandstand.

"Come on," I said after a while. "They're going to start the walk soon."

Near the starting line, Amber stopped short.

"Oh. My. God."

I followed her gaze. Near us stood two figures. They were tall—wearing clingy, flashy clothes, and they were super curvy. They looked like women, but both were broader and more imposing than any woman I'd ever seen.

"Drag queens!" Amber whispered. Her eyes sparkled with delight.

I smiled at her. Yep, she was right. Men dressed as women— something I'd seen only on television at that point. They seemed larger than life somehow. Glamorous and confident. Each wore a sash, just like a beauty pageant winner. One had on formfitting silver sparkle pants and a black feather boa. The other wore a bright red tracksuit, her hair swept back into a gorgeous blond updo. Both wore heels, so much makeup it was almost hard to see their eyes, and sparkly tiaras that glittered in the sun.

I read their sashes: The ribbon on the one in the track suit said MISS GAY INDIANA. The one in the boa read MISS GAY MUNCIE, INDIANA.

I couldn't help but feel in awe of them—standing there chatting, so comfortable with themselves, when who they were was so *different*. I wished I had just a tiny little piece of their confidence—that sense of pride.

My mom must have seen the admiring look on my face. "Paige!" she exclaimed. "Go get a picture with them!"

"Oh, Mom, they wouldn't want . . ."

But before I could get further, my mom was already waving to them. "Hey, my daughter's a pageant winner, too!"

"Mom," I hissed. I was mortified.

But they came over right away, smiling and laughing. They asked me about which pageants I'd been in, and they congratulated me on my wins. While we talked, my mom lifted her camera. "Smile, everyone!" she cried.

Without missing a beat, they draped their arms around me. The top of my head barely reached Miss Gay Indiana's chest. But standing between them made me feel safe in a way I couldn't quite explain. Safer than I could remember feeling in a long, long time. I laughed out loud as my mom snapped a few photos.

When we said good-bye, all of us waving happily, I realized something: I was better having met them than I had been before. All of us seemed better—more at ease—*uplifted*. There is something enormously freeing, I realized, about spending time with people who are totally unafraid to be themselves.

The walk itself wasn't long. We headed south on Meridian Street, onto the east side of the canal, then we looped back again, back toward the Memorial and the booths and the quilt panels. People clapped and cheered and whistled for us the whole way along. It was five kilometers, about three miles.

My memories of those miles are mostly fragmented images: a young man wearing a T-shirt—*Living and loving life*. An older woman with white hair pulled back in a bun who carried a sign that said simply, *Miss you every day.* An older man standing at the side, high-fiving us as we passed. Dogs in red sweaters that trotted alongside the walkers.

I remember my mom pink-cheeked and breathing hard in the hot sun. Erin and Amber laughing, like this was all normal. Erin with a red ribbon tattoo stuck on her cheek.

What I remember most of all, though, isn't so much an image. It's a feeling. A feeling of waking up. It was, I realized, as if I'd been in a kind of slumber, and now my eyes were opening.

So many people judged me for this thing—this virus that lived inside me through no fault of my own. Yet here, in this crazy crowd of men dressed like women, pets in rainbow tutus, people remembering, people celebrating, people with broken hearts, and people determined to fight, nobody had a problem with me. If they noticed me at all, they seemed to accept me—for exactly who I was.

I might have been an outcast at Clarkstown. But I wasn't now. Not here.

As we crossed the finish line, cheerleaders shook pom-poms and cheered for us.

"G! O! G! O! Go, go go!" For a moment, I cheered back.

Although I still missed being a cheerleader, I had to admit: just for this moment, it was nice to have someone cheer *for me.*

I thought about that card I'd dropped in my bag—the one from the Women in Motion group.

It might be nice, I thought. *It might be nice to tell my story one of these days.*

*Being at the AIDS Walk was freeing—no one looked at me differently
just because of my diagnosis. And for the first time in a long time
I thought maybe there was a place where I could feel like I belonged.*

· · ·

Two months later, I stood in front of a small crowd at a Teen
Extravaganza talent show. It was a big, open room. Two
hundred people, nearly all of them strangers, sat in folding
chairs. They were waiting for me to speak.

I was terrified.

It started on the drive.

"What's the matter, Paige?" my mom had asked. "You've
won pageants. You know how to talk in front of a crowd."

She didn't understand. She didn't understand that pageants
were a kind of show. They weren't real. The questions—
caboose or engine?—were just for fun.

At pageants, I got to be in control. I got to look strong and
optimistic.

At a pageant, I didn't have to stand up and say things like *I
have a disease.*

Or, *Because of that, I lost friends.*

Or, *People hurt me.*

Or, *Everything feels totally out of control.*

I didn't have to admit my truth. And that was what I'd be admitting tonight. That I had a disease. That people had hurt me. And that I didn't have it all under control.

As I stood backstage, waiting for my spot in the program, I watched kids I didn't know belt out tunes into a microphone. They performed hip-hop routines, recited their own poetry. Elsewhere in the room, the AIDS Ministry Network tested for HIV and handed out brochures on different diseases.

All of that was kind of a blur. Because all I could really focus on was the piece of paper—just one sheet—that I was clutching with my shaking hands. I scanned the crowd for the few faces I knew: my mom; Amber; the woman, Marie, who I'd met at the AIDS Walk.

I took deep ragged breaths and told myself quietly to stay calm. Then, I stepped up to the microphone.

I remember hearing my voice crack as I spoke.

"I'm Paige Rawl," I began. "I'm fourteen years old, and I am affected by something called HIV."

I didn't—I couldn't—look up as I told the rest of my story: the loss of friends, the teachers and administrators who didn't seem to care, the bullying, the seizures.

The room was quiet.

And then I remember this: when it was done people began applauding. I looked out into the crowd, and I felt a weight lifted, a weight I hadn't even known I was carrying.

I remember feeling like maybe I didn't have anything to hide.

Herron High

*Herron High was amazing. I felt safe and supported there.
But I was still struggling with what I had been through,
and I don't think anyone realized it—not even me.*

I visited Herron High School for the first time during my eighth-grade year.

I'd been home with my mom, day after day, for nearly a year. I'd studied history alone, taken tests alone, calculated fractions and percentages alone, conjugated verbs alone, and learned about the food chain alone.

I saw a few friends on weekends. I saw Erin and Mariah and Amber, a handful of others, when they weren't busy with school stuff.

But most of the time—at least five days a week, week after week and month after month—though, I'd been alone.

Some things were better; I hadn't had another seizure since I'd left Clarkstown. I slept better at night. I had stopped cutting myself, stopped grinding my teeth, and my stomach pains were almost gone.

But it wasn't enough for me. It wasn't nearly enough. I longed to laugh with friends, to be a part of something, to see other people—to see something other than the walls of my house— when I looked up from my notebook. I wanted to play sports, to cheerlead, to sing and dance. I wanted something other than me and my mom, this house, this sofa, this television, this stack of books.

I'd heard about Herron from a family member, and it sounded like an altogether different kind of school experience. *A public charter school*, their website said. *A classical, liberal arts education that integrates knowledge, inspires character, and values community service.*

I knew they had an advanced concert choir, and I'd loved to sing since I was small. So there was that. Mostly, though, I read these words over and over: *Knowledge. Character. Community.*

I emphasized the last word especially. *Community.*

The school building, in downtown Indianapolis, was the former Indianapolis Museum of Art. It looked like a museum, too—high ceilings, grand staircase, windows and marble everywhere. Touring it the first time, I whispered to my mom that it looked like a school you'd find in New York City. Or London, or Paris.

It felt like it was a million miles from Clarkstown.

I noticed things on that visit. I noticed that kids didn't seem to circle into tight groups; they moved around more openly. Everyone interacted with everyone else.

I noticed that all the teachers had small statues on their desks, tiny ancient-looking busts. I sat in on a Latin class, and listened to the teacher weave deftly between conjugating verbs and

Greek mythology, waving his arms the whole while. I loved it. On the way out of class, I glanced at the statue that was on top of his desk—the bust of someone I did not recognize. He noticed me looking at it.

"That's Aristotle," he said. "You know much about Aristotle?"

I shook my head and picked up the statue.

"He believed in character. In virtue."

I nodded as if I understood. The teacher continued, "He believed in education, in using knowledge to become our best selves. What do you think about that?"

I shrugged. I looked at the bust for a long time before setting it down. Then I looked up at him. "I think maybe not enough people do that."

He laughed. "You'll also find statues of Plato, Shakespeare, a bunch of the others. Every year we get a different one. They remind us to make our mark in this world, to think about what's right."

I nodded and started to leave the room. He called after me.

"Hey, Paige?"

I turned around.

"I hope to see you back here."

He seemed to mean it.

And that was another thing: the way the Herron teachers interacted with the students felt different from anything I'd ever seen. They were more relaxed with the students, but also more caring. They looked the kids in the eye. They looked *me* in the eye.

It felt homey, this school. Homey and challenging both. Maybe, I thought, there was a school for me, after all.

Later, my mom and I sat down with Ms. Lane, the assistant to Herron High School's head of school. She was a serious woman—friendly enough, but without a fake smile plastered across her face.

I liked that. I no longer trusted plastered smiles.

My mom, I could tell, was nervous. She began explaining to Ms. Lane what had happened to me at Clarkstown. Ms. Lane listened, occasionally turning to me with a smile.

"Paige just had a lot of problems at her old school," my mom said, the words coming out in a rush. "She had a lot of friends, and then something happened, and she started to get bullied."

Ms. Lane nodded. "I'm sorry to hear that. I want you to know that we don't tolerate bullying at Herron."

"I mean," my mother continued, "it's like she was one of them, one of the gang, and then they turned on her. They were like a pack of animals, the way they turned on one of their own."

Ms. Lane nodded and opened her mouth as if she was about to say something, but my mother kept talking. "It wasn't the kids you'd expect, either," she said. "These were the so-called good kids. The honor roll students. The ones from good homes. But they were just heartless. Totally merciless. And nobody did anything. The school didn't—"

"Mrs. Rawl—"

"And then they just let Paige leave. They said they couldn't promise to protect her. It was like they'd given up and—"

"That must have been—"

"So now she's at home, she hasn't been able to do the things she loves to do, she's not challenged, and I just can't believe—"

"Mrs. Rawl." Ms. Lane's voice was absolutely calm. "I want to assure you that Herron does not tolerate—"

"Nothing was ever done. Nobody ever got punished. What she needs—"

"Mom," I jumped in.

"Is a school where—"

"Mom."

"She knows she can be safe from—"

"Mom."

My mother looked up.

I glanced at Ms. Lane, who looked my mom right in the eye. "We don't tolerate bullying at Herron, Mrs. Rawl," she repeated.

My mom let that sink in. She frowned. "But it's kids. So how do you . . . ?" She stopped and frowned.

"We just don't tolerate it. Kids rise to the expectations that are set for them. It really is that simple."

My mother glanced back and forth. For a moment she looked confused, then her shoulders visibly relaxed. "Well, okay," she said. "Okay. Good," she said.

So it can be that simple, I thought. *You just don't tolerate it.*

Mom reached into her purse and pulled out the article from the *Indianapolis Star*—the one about me, about the lawsuit. Up until this point, she still hadn't told Ms. Lane about my HIV. But she handed the article to Ms. Lane. "You should know," she said. "This is her. This story is about Paige."

Ms. Lane read it for a few moments, then she looked up. She looked me right in the eye.

"I'm sorry this happened to you," she said. "It won't happen here."

Her voice was so confident. Just completely certain.

The lawsuit had been dragging on. It wasn't hard to notice how angry my mother was every time our attorney called. She would scream into the phone each time, "They said WHAT?" and "That's not how it happened at all!" Then she would hang up the phone, and I'd pester her with questions.

Eventually, she would tell me.

The school's attorney is suggesting that your seizures weren't from stress, that they were actually because you hit your head during that cheerleading fall.

(*Whaaat?* I'd scream. *They did an MRI. My head was fine. I didn't even have a concussion. And how do you explain the fact that the seizures stopped when I left Clarkstown?*)

Or she'd say: *I don't know, honey, they're claiming they never got those notes I left for Miss Fischer.*

(Then me: *You're kidding me, right? They're either lying or completely incompetent, Mom.*)

Then Mom would sigh and I would march out of the room and sit in the bathroom with music on, or inside my bedroom with arms folded.

But now, sitting at Herron, Ms. Lane held the newspaper article about me. She had just reassured me: it won't happen here. And the contrast of it all—her assurance that "it won't happen here," versus Miss Fischer's weak, old "I cannot promise to keep you safe"—was dramatic.

Ms. Lane turned to my mom. "Thank you for sharing this with me. Do you mind if I make a copy?"

My mother shook her head. "No, I guess not."

Ms. Lane nodded, stood, and left the room for a moment.

I turned to look at my mother. "I think this is it," I said. "I think I love it here."

Later, once my enrollment was complete, Mom and I visited with the Herron High School nurse. It was still summer, but my mom wanted to discuss my medicines. She wanted to explain about the seizures, in case they should start happening again.

While my mom and the nurse talked, I glanced around the

office. My eyes fell onto a white plastic bag sitting next to her desk. It had a red ribbon on the outside, with the words INDIANA AIDS FUND printed on the front. I walked over to the bag and picked it up. It was filled with pamphlets.

The nurse smiled at me. "I picked up a bunch of information," she said. "I just wanted to make sure we are doing everything possible to accommodate a student with HIV."

My mother practically gaped at the nurse. "You did that?"

"Of course I did," the nurse said, a little surprised by my mother's reaction. "As a school, we need to be as informed as possible," she said. She glanced at me, then looked back at my mom.

"It's our responsibility," she said very matter-of-factly. "Paige is now one of our students.

"I mean," she added almost as an afterthought, "it's only if we learn all we can that we'll be able to lead our students in learning all they can."

I thought back two years, to the time I sat in Miss Ward's office, when she told me to deny having HIV. I remembered her face, so bright and chipper, as if denying my status were the best idea since sliced bread.

And in that moment, in the nurse's office, I finally understood what I wished Miss Ward had done that day.

There were so many things she could have done, after all. Miss Ward could have said, "Thank you for choosing to share that with me." She could have said, "I'm so sorry you are struggling with this." Or maybe even, "How can we support you?"

And if she didn't know to say these things, she could have said, "I don't know very much about HIV, I don't know exactly how I should handle this, but I will learn more."

Above all, that's what I wished Miss Ward had done: I

wished she had decided to learn something. I mean, maybe she wasn't sure about what it means to support a kid with HIV. But it seemed so simple now: she should have learned about it so that she could lead others.

She could have showed a little bit of bravery, a little bit of leadership.

I remembered her face, that wide bright smile that offered no help whatsoever. I hated her. I swear to God, I hated Miss Ward, just like I hated everyone I had left behind.

The very thought of them made me bitter.

I looked at my mom then, who was standing there with the nurse. Mom's eyes were welling up with tears. I knew she felt relieved—relieved that at last, she didn't feel alone.

I walked over to her, and she smiled at me, such a warm and happy smile. If I could have bottled that smile, I would have. I would have bottled it and put it in a jar, so I could take it out the next time I needed a little extra warmth. I leaned my head against her shoulder, and she kissed me on top of the head.

Herron was so hopeful, right from the start.

And that feeling that I had—that it was the place for me— was correct.

It was the right place. It was—it is—a good place.

But.

But there were some things I didn't understand, not yet.

I didn't understand that everything that had already happened—the name-calling, the notes, that desperate sense that everything around me was out of control, that increasing isolation from my friends, that year of desperate aloneness— had taken deep root in me.

I didn't understand that their effects were inside of me, almost like a virus.

I didn't understand that a change in scenery—even to a good place, to a welcoming place, to a place that was doing everything it could to accommodate me—wouldn't be enough to undo some of what had been done.

There was darkness inside me. It would be inside of me for a while longer.

Herron couldn't push out the darkness. Ms. Lane couldn't. The school nurse couldn't. Aristotle couldn't.

Only I could do that.

And I wasn't ready to do it. Not yet. Not by a long shot.

Escape

Sometimes, the biggest moments in your life happen with no thought at all.

It was September. Ninth grade. I'd been at Herron High School for a month; nothing bad had happened.

Better than that, I liked it.

I'd started late. Just before Labor Day, I'd gotten a bad case of meningitis. My fever had spiked, my head and neck ached. This was no ordinary illness—it came on in a rush, and by the day's end I was in the hospital.

By the time I had come home, all the other Herron students, all my future classmates, already knew their way around the halls.

It made me extra nervous to start—already, I was an outsider, and I hadn't even started—but my mother had looked me in the eye and told me not to be afraid.

"You're going to like Herron, Paige," she said. "I really think you will."

And now the meningitis was gone, and my mother had been right. I did like it.

I liked that the school displayed student art everywhere inside the buildings. I liked the buildings themselves—the scrollwork moldings and iron fences up and down marble stairs, and the lofty feeling that museum architecture gave me.

I liked that I could sit with anyone at lunch, that I could approach anyone in the hallway. I like that I never once felt left out.

I liked the way teachers talked to us—like we were people, adults even, not young children. I liked how that made me feel like I could do anything.

I liked my classes, liked being one of twenty-something kids in a classroom, all opening up to the same page in the same workbook at the same time.

I liked not feeling alone.

But.

Outside of school, my mom and I were hurtling toward a settlement hearing. All these meetings with attorneys, all of those phone calls, all of the talk, this endless talk, about what had happened at Clarkstown had started to wear on me. I didn't understand why it had to be so complicated.

I just wanted to shout at everyone: *This is what happened at Clarkstown! It happened like I'm telling you!*

It made me feel like no one believed me, like I was just making the whole thing up.

So there was the meningitis, and there was the lawsuit. But I swear, it wasn't just the meningitis, and wasn't just the settlement hearing, and it certainly wasn't Herron.

Something else was wrong.

There had been signs, I realize now. Like the first day of Herron soccer practice, for example. I'd gotten so nervous that I started shaking. Then I vomited and had to be helped to my mom's car.

I told people I must have a stomach bug.

There were other things, too. I was crying a lot these days, breaking down for no reason. Sometimes I found it hard to breathe. Everything felt like it was coming just a little too close, somehow, the world closing in around me, the air so stuffy I might suffocate.

And there were other moments, different moments, but no

less strange. Moments when I felt that strange disconnection from myself. Moments when I felt like I was moving without thought, moving automatically. Moving toward something specific. Like right now.

It was evening. My mother was in the kitchen, watching television. We had just finished dinner.

I walked into the bathroom. My feet stepped in front of me, simple as anything: one, two, three, four. There, in the bathroom, were my mom's floral towels. They were brown and turquoise, folded neatly in squares. There was the matching shower curtain and bath mat. There was the hair dryer hanging on a hook next to the sink. There, on the counter, was an empty glass. Jars of hand soap and cocoa butter lotion, each positioned just so on the sink, angled like two armchairs in a living room. Or maybe a psychiatrist's office.

I closed the door behind me. Behind the door, I saw it: the cabinet, the white bathroom cabinet, just a little taller than myself.

I opened it.

Sometimes everything you see around you is like a still life, like a snapshot you've tacked to the inside of your locker, or a painting pinned on a bulletin board. You have come to know it so well, that still life, that it almost seems this moment in time has always existed, side by side with all those other experiences you've had.

There was the Ajax cleaner on the bottom shelf, next to the Band-Aids and gauze, the antiperspirant and Caress soap. Above it, peroxide, hair mousse, Halls cough drops, and Listerine. And on the shelf above that, the spare tubes of toothpaste, the pink basket full of nail polish, the Q-tips.

I wondered briefly if anyone ever really finishes a box of Q-tips, if they ever pull a single, final Q-tip from the box.

I stopped to wonder that. So it's not like I was not thinking at all.

It was the very top shelf that drew my eye. That was where the medicine was stored. The medicine, all that stupid medicine: the horse pills that I swallowed every day, that my mother took, too, in our attempts to save our own lives. And there were other medicines: the pills I took to make me hungry, so I could actually keep a few pounds on, finish the pudding cups my mom was always handing to me. There were the pills I had taken for what I now called my "Clarkstown-induced seizures." There were the ones my mom took for the occasional panic attack, when the stress of caring for me, for trying to keep us alive, became too much.

None of those pills were the ones I wanted.

My hand reached up. It moved without me, like it belonged to someone else. It reached for the other pills, the ones with my mother's name on them, the ones she took to help her get to sleep at night.

Sleeping pills.

I had seen these pills. Had seen the warnings.

I shook out a handful. How many were there? I didn't care. I knew only that it was as many as I was able to hold. I put the plastic container down with my right hand, turned on the water. I picked up the glass next to the faucet, filled it with water.

Then one by one, I swallowed the pills, counting as I went.

One.

Two.

Three.

Four.

And on until I hit fifteen. One for every year I had been alive.

I was good at taking pills—better than any kid I knew.

It took under a minute to swallow them. It wasn't anything at all.

I looked into the mirror and stared back at myself. The light above the sink flickered ever so slightly. I put the cap back on the medicine bottle, placed it back on the shelf, and closed the cabinet.

I sat down on the edge of the bathtub and waited. I had the strangest sensation that all of this was happening to someone else. It was as if none of it was real.

At first, nothing.

After a minute or two: still nothing. The bathroom light hummed.

And then I noticed my eyelids. They were heavy.

And before long (how much time? Ten minutes? Twenty?), I was tired.

A little longer (how much longer? I really couldn't tell anymore): I was really, really tired.

I stood up. I wanted sleep. The light was humming so loudly, and there were other sounds, too. There was the sound of the door opening, the knob snapping back in place. There was the sound of my own footsteps walking toward my bedroom, of my mother opening a drawer in the next room. There was all that light and color. It was too much light, too much color.

It was too much, all of it. I wanted to shut my eyes.

The world had a problem, I realized: it was so noisy, and there were so many things to think about. Sleep was the answer. Sleep sounded so good, so calming.

In sleep, I wouldn't have to think about settlement hearings. In sleep, I wouldn't have to be afraid of running into a group of kids in my own hometown. In sleep, I never had to explain myself.

I could just quiet all that noise. Lie down. Make it disappear.

I closed the door to my room and lay down on the bed. I heard the television in the kitchen. My mother was watching a news show, or maybe it was a celebrity news show, which was not really the same thing. Someone famous had checked into rehab. I didn't care who it was. It didn't matter, anyway; all of it was just so much noise.

I should tell my mother, I thought. I should tell her how sleep would just quiet all of that down. *She could use some quiet, too,* I thought.

I looked up at the ceiling and wondered if it was starting to spin, or if I was imagining that.

I closed my eyes, and the world began to fade away.

Then I sat up. I sat up straight and suddenly. I stood, which turned out to be surprisingly difficult: it was like I was trying to control someone else's arms and legs.

I walked to the door, reached for the knob. Yes, I thought. This was the knob. I felt it in my hand, round and hard and slightly cold. Just turn. I walked out of my room and into the kitchen.

Forming a word was hard. It took thought. *Lips are so strange when they don't work right.*

"Mom?"

She leaned against the counter, her eyes on the television. "Mmm?"

"Mom, I think I did something stupid."

She must have heard it in my voice, because she looked at me immediately. Her face changed. Her eyes flickered all over me. I didn't know eyes could dart around so quickly.

"What?" Her voice was almost a whisper. There was something in it I had never heard. *Panic,* the disconnected part of my brain thought. *That is the sound of panic.*

And then. *Oh, no, I've done it again. I've gone and worried her.* I was always worrying her.

"What did you do, Paige?"

"Mom?" I didn't want to scare her. But that thing I'd heard in her voice had started welling up in me. "Mom?" I sounded like a little child, my own voice very far away.

She rushed over to me. "Oh, God, Paige, what did you do? What did you do?"

"I took the pills." My words were so slow.

A whisper. "Oh, God."

"I think I need to go to the hospital, Mom."

She grabbed me, picked up her keys. She pulled me toward the garage. She left the TV on, the lights on. We were leaving a lit and loud house, heading out into the night.

"Oh, God, Paige. Oh, God. Oh, God."

And just like that, she was pushing me into her car, clicking my belt for me, her hands fumbling. And then we were making the drive that I already knew so well—downtown, to Riley.

She was asking questions, so many questions.

"What kind, honey? What kind of pills?"

"Trazodone."

"How many?"

Silence. It was so tiring, forming words.

"How many, Paige? Tell me how many!" Her voice was loud now.

I noticed how white her fingers were; she was gripping the wheel hard. I noticed that.

"Fifteen," I said. My voice could barely be heard over the car engine. Still, I heard her suck in her breath.

She drove fast, faster than she ever drives. But time was all different now, the way it could feel fast and slow, all at once. It was like the car was in one time zone and I was in a different one.

We swayed from side to side, and everything rushed past us way too fast. It was hard to keep my eyes focused on anything, and I really just wanted to rest my head and close my eyes. I didn't think it would be too bad if I closed my eyes, as long as I did it only for a minute. But every time I rested my head against the car window, we hit a bump and my head banged against the glass.

"Stay awake, Paige!" She was screaming now. She reached over with one hand, grabbed my arm, and shook me. "Honey, you can't do this. You can't do this. You can't let them win. It's not worth it."

I couldn't quite focus on her words. There were so many of them, and they were coming at me so fast.

"Why would you do this?" she asked, though I know she wasn't really looking for an answer.

"Oh, Paige." Then she glanced over at me again. "Stay awake, Paige! Jesus, just stay awake!"

And then we were in the parking lot, and she threw on the brake. She was moving so quickly. Somehow she was already outside the car, opening my door, and yanking me up. "Come on."

She started pulling me. I stood, but nothing in my body was working right. It was like moving underwater somehow.

And then she was screaming to no one, to everyone, "Help us! It's an emergency. Oh, God, somebody help us!"

It was like a scene from a TV movie, the kind of movie that my mom and I might watch together, staying up later than we should, both of us sniffling and wiping tears from our eyes at the end. Except that in this case I was inside the movie, and my mother was, too. It was so odd, because the movie was happening all around me.

And then in an instant, there was a team of people around

me, and my mother was there, and then she wasn't. And it didn't matter that I was so tired, and it didn't matter that my lips wouldn't move right. I was in the parking lot, and then there were the sliding doors, and then there was a nurse, and then I was in a bright room.

One person after another came in the room, and they asked questions, they just kept asking so many questions, and it was so hard to keep track of who was who.

And I spent that first night at Riley so they could monitor my heart. I was under suicide watch, which meant I was not allowed to be alone, not even to go to the bathroom.

But I was too worn out to care.

God, I was just so tired.

Bright lights. White coats. People in scrubs. Why do all the people in a hospital dress alike? You can barely tell who is the janitor and who is the doctor.

They came in, they went out.

They gave me a terrible-tasting black drink, which made my stomach cramp painfully.

I heard murmurs.

Activated charcoal. Irregular heartbeat. Possible organ damage.

I vomited in a bucket, again and again.

Really quite serious.

I slept, I woke up. Someone's hands were on me. I closed my eyes, and when I opened them that person was gone, and another person was there.

My mother was there. Then she wasn't. Then she was again. Here. Gone. Here. Gone. Talking-which-was-murmuring. Flickering lights. The hum of these lights reminded me of the hum in the bathroom.

How long ago was that? An hour? A day? A lifetime, maybe.

Somewhere during that night, one of the staff members asked me, "Were you actually trying to kill yourself?" And I must have been starting to feel like myself again, because I knew, right then, what the answer to his question was.

Maybe.

Maybe, if that's what it took for it all to stop. One way or another, I wanted it all—the comments, the loneliness, the terrible way I felt about myself, the fear that it would never get better—to just stop.

I turned away from him and faced the wall.

In the morning, Dr. Cox came in to see me. I was back in my right mind by then, more in control.

I was in control enough to imagine her getting the phone call—*Paige Rawl is in the hospital after a suicide attempt*, someone must have said. I thought about all she had done for me, all the work she put into keeping me alive and healthy, all those years.

I felt ashamed. I once thought it would be impossible to feel shame with Dr. Cox.

". . . no permanent damage," Dr. Cox was saying. ". . . going to be okay."

No permanent damage.

I closed my eyes.

"I thought it was better, Paige," Dr. Cox said quietly. "I thought things were getting better."

"They are," I said. "That's the funny thing."

And I wanted to explain it to her—that sense of wanting it all to stop.

There were a million different things I wanted to stop. There was the fear that things wouldn't stay better, that things at Herron would turn bad, just the way everything turned so terrible at Clarkstown. There was the sheer exhaustion that followed my bout with meningitis. The shock about having been hospitalized like that, and so suddenly. There was the stress of the lawsuit, the attorney's questions, that sense of having to defend myself when the people who hurt me were just going about their lives.

Meanwhile, who knew what effects all that medicine would have: the HIV drugs that kept me alive, or the antidepressants that countered the effects of the HIV drugs, or the drugs I took to boost the appetite that I never had as a result of the HIV drugs. Who knew how they might interact inside my body?

But mostly, I knew what my mom had said in the car was true: those kids at Clarkstown had gotten inside me somehow. They'd gotten really deep inside me, turned me against myself, just like a tiny spiked virus had turned the cells that were supposed to protect me into the very things that were trying to kill me.

I wanted them out. Gone. Whatever it took.

Soon after, I was getting into an ambulance—so many ambulances already, and I was just fifteen years old. I was looking at the medical equipment that helps keep people alive in the most dire of emergencies. The sky above me disappeared, and the doors closed behind me, and then I was heading across town. We moved slowly, not like the times that I woke up in speeding ambulances after my seizures.

Riley, the hospital that I knew so well, almost my second home, was behind me. Somewhere ahead of me was something they called a "stress center" just for teens, which a nurse was telling me was a safe environment.

And to keep it that way, they would lock the door behind me and take away my sneakers and belt.

Stress Center

The first thing I remember about the Northside Pavilion is SpongeBob.

I was standing in a big room, the day room, where a flickery television showed cartoons. On the screen in front of me, Squidward was trying to teach SpongeBob and a bunch of other sea creatures how to play musical instruments. When the characters blew into their instruments, bubbles floated out.

There were a few kids in the room, scattered at tables. They sat staring at the set. No one was laughing.

It was evening by now. I'd spent all day answering questions: *And how are you feeling now? Are you hearing any voices? Medications?* My mom had been there for much of that, by my side as always, until a nurse told her it was time to go.

Don't go, I said, clinging to her. *Please don't leave me here.* I didn't know what this place was. I just knew it wasn't home. I cried fat, bitter tears onto her shoulder.

The nurse watched me with my arms around my mom like I was a young child. She heard my sobs—choking sobs, the kind that make it hard to catch your breath. Her face didn't change at all. She showed no surprise, no distaste. And that's when I knew that a stress center was different from school. A stress center was the kind of place where sadness wasn't hidden away. People saw sadness so much that at a certain point it didn't even faze them anymore.

My mom stroked the back of my head and held me as long as she could. Then when the nurse said, "Mrs. Rawl," Mom sort of pushed me away and rushed to the door without looking back. I knew how sad and worried she must be.

I walked through the door, which clicked behind me when it shut. My knees felt so weak I thought I might pass out.

I wanted to. I wanted to drop to the floor right then and there.

Just yesterday I had been doing homework. But now my mom was leaving, and I was stuck here, on the wrong side of the door that clicked.

Pajama bottoms and sweatpants seemed to be the fashion items of choice, I noted as I looked around the day room. I didn't see a single mirror in the room—not even any pictures in frames— and all these kids in their old T-shirts looked like they'd never smiled in their lives. I looked at one kid, an enormous boy, wide and tall, wearing flip-flops, basketball shorts, and a wide Cookie Monster T-shirt. He probably weighed as much as four of me, and he just sat there, his back rounded, staring into the ground, slack-jawed.

No way, I thought. *There's no way this is real. I'm not really here with these people.* I swear, I had this feeling that I might get swallowed up by their sorrow.

Cookie Monster glanced up at me and nodded in greeting. I looked away.

That's when I heard a voice behind me.

"Oh, thank God *you're* here," the voice said. It was a boy's voice, but it had inflections more like a girl's. I turned around and saw a skinny kid with dark skin walking toward me. He grabbed my arm. It was like he knew me, although I was certain I had never seen him in my life. "You're one of the normal ones, right? Thank God, because I was just about to die from the stultifying depressing-ness of this whole affair," he whispered.

Okay. Okay, I could survive anything—maybe even this—as long as I had a friend.

A day at a stress center is spent shuffling between meetings—group sessions and coping sessions and goal-setting sessions that are supposed to help you imagine other possibilities.

At my first group meeting, a leader named Brendan asked kids introduce themselves—first names only, plus age and why we were here. There were about ten of us altogether, and we sat in a circle in a corner of the day room.

I learned that the boy who'd grabbed my arm—his name was Louis—lived in a small town about forty-five miles away. His parents were religious, they didn't understand him, and he didn't understand them. At school, he'd been beaten up a bunch of times, because everyone thought he was gay.

"I might be," he said, shifting in his seat. "But I'm not telling."

Then he looked right at me and nodded dramatically, mouthing the words, "I am," as if everyone in the room couldn't see it. I surprised myself by laughing, then stopped myself. This didn't seem like the kind of place where one should laugh.

Louis said that he also had struggled with bulimia in the past, that he had severe anxiety attacks, and what his mother gently called mood swings, which actually meant some days being completely unable to get out of bed.

Yeah, I thought. *Yeah, I know what that's like.*

After a moment, another person broke the silence. "I'm Stacy." That came from a girl with straight, jet-black hair. She looked around. "Frequent flyer here. OCD. Depression. Self-harm." She folded her arms across her chest. "I'm having the time of my life. It's like a fucking *Seventeen* magazine photo spread, being me."

There were other stories, too: a fourteen-year-old who had been raped by a family member, a Goth boy whose anxiety attacks got worse after his dad was shipped to Afghanistan. (*The hardest part,* he said, *is knowing that he's over there worried about me.*) Another girl—a thin, preppy-looking girl, the kind you'd expect to see on the tennis team—said nothing at all. She wore a long sweatshirt and gripped the cuffed ends of the sleeves in her fists. I remembered doing that, and I wondered what was on her wrists.

I gave the basic outline of my own story. Paige. Fifteen years old. HIV. Bullied. Stacy flashed hard eyes at me and scoffed, "You have HIV? Why are you even *in here* with us?" She said it like I should be quarantined, and I was like, *Okay, you mean I'm not even good enough for here?*

Brendan stopped her. "Stacy, there's no risk to you from Paige's HIV."

And while he was speaking, Louis met my eye and pointed ever so slightly at Stacy, then made a gagging face.

So not *everyone* wanted to make me an outcast. That made me feel a tiny bit better.

"Paige," Brendan said. "These guys have heard it before, but at Northside Pavilion we use a strength-based model of care. We want you to identify your own strengths, so you can use them in your own recovery."

I nodded along. But I was thinking, *In the last fifteen minutes, just listening to these stories, I think I already found some strengths.*

Unlike some of these other kids, I had no addictions, no history of molestation, no hallucinations, no psychosis, no compulsive, violent outbursts.

By the standards of the locked-door facility of the stress center, I was doing pretty okay.

. . .

That was a word that came up often, it turned out. *Okay.*

In all these meetings, we talked about how we were feeling, and that was always our answer. *Okay,* we'd say, one after another. *I'm okay.*

Okay, I guess.

I dunno. I'm okay.

And then usually someone would cry, because none of us were really okay. If we had been okay, we wouldn't have been there in the first place, wouldn't have been seated in a circle inside that room. We wouldn't have had staff checking on us every fifteen minutes; we wouldn't be wearing pants whose drawstrings had been carefully pulled out from the waist.

We'd be out in the sunshine, or at a basketball game, or at the mall, or at school. We would be in the unbroken world, surrounded by those who still seemed whole.

We didn't have to dress well. We didn't have to brush our hair. We didn't have to do homework, or put on sports uniforms, or smile at other people in the hallway. We didn't have to smile at all, or be happy, or make grown-ups feel good about themselves. We just had to show up, exactly as we were.

When you bottom out, and that is exactly what I had done, it turns out people don't expect much.

We had sessions, one after another, when we had to do exercises like "write one negative thought, then three positive ones."

My negative: *I am in a stress center because I took too many pills.*

My positives:

1. *I am wearing my favorite socks, which my mom brought me, even though I wasn't allowed to see her.*
2. *I like when they play music in the day room and let us sit quietly.*
3. *This morning I thought about that Aristotle statue.*

In another session, we circled our positive traits from a work sheet (me: *accepting, self-directed, open-minded*; Louis: *sensitive, realistic, goofy*, plus *attractive* circled three times with arrows). In another, we identified triggers for our stress (me: *anything having to do with Clarkstown*; Louis: *absolutely everything*. Stacy: *this hellhole*. Tennis girl: *people judging me*).

And I know what I'm supposed to say: I know I'm supposed to say that I hated being locked in there, that the nurses were awful, disconnected, and dictatorial, that everyone inside was a raging maniac, and that I just couldn't wait to get out of there. But the truth is, it turned out to not be that bad. More than that, I think it *helped*.

Sometimes Louis made me laugh, and sometimes Stacy looked at us and rolled her eyes, but sometimes it was in a friendly way.

My second day there, she sat down on the couch next to me and said, "I can be a bitch sometimes. It's part of my problem. Sorry about that."

I shrugged. "That's okay."

And it kind of was.

Even the Cookie Monster guy, who mostly just looked down at his feet, had moments of kindness, like one morning, when tennis girl knocked over a bowl of Cheerios with the back of her hand. The cereal had spilled all over the kid next to her (fourteen, ADHD, Tourette's, mood swings, possible bipolar). One of the nurses came over to her and spoke to her in a low voice. I could not hear what she was saying.

"I'm just having a really freaking hard time," Tennis sobbed to the nurse.

And while she cried, Cookie Monster stood up, got a bunch of towels, and began silently mopping it all up.

I'm telling you: it was the most visibly broken assortment of human beings I'd ever been around. But I don't know. Maybe being broken helps you understand others' brokenness. Maybe being broken helps you become a better person.

"So let me get this straight," said Louis. It was mealtime, and we were waiting in line for our trays of food, which had been brought up from the cafeteria. Near us, at a table, Tennis was picking at chicken with her spoon. "I'm gay, and kids say that I have AIDS, even though I don't. And you're the straightest, skinniest little white girl I've ever met, *and* you're a beauty queen, and you actually do have AIDS."

"Not AIDS," I said. "HIV."

"Yeah, I know, HIV," he said, waving his hand with a little flourish. It was his turn for food, so he stepped up to the nurse in charge.

"Name and birthday?" she asked. It was a question we had to answer every single time they gave us food, every time we took medicine. He answered in a bored tone of voice. Louis Mitchell, 7/18/93. She handed him a tray.

"But isn't that a little crazy?" he asked, still talking to me. "I mean, doesn't it all seem backward?"

My turn. "Paige Rawl. August 11, 1994."

She handed me my tray. Pizza.

I shrugged. "I guess."

"It's ass-backward is what it is," he said, sitting down.

"Actually," I told him, "I heard Clarkstown's lawyer is suggesting I might be gay, too." I'd already told Louis all about the lawsuit, about the lawyer's calls, about the fact that there would be a settlement hearing in just a few days.

"What, huh?" he asked. He looked surprised, then he said, "No. Wait, give me a moment. I want to do an actual spit take." He took a swig of water from his glass, glanced around the room, then quickly spat it back out, spraying water against the wall in a dramatic show of shock. I glanced at the staff, but no one seemed to have noticed.

Then he continued. "So . . . what now? They think you're gay?"

I shrugged. "Not really. But they subpoenaed my texts. In some of them I called my friends 'sweetie.' So my mom says that now they're claiming that maybe I'm gay. That's the last thing I heard, anyway."

"But—why?"

"So they can say that that's the true cause of my stress. Not the bullying, but that I'm stressed out from hiding that I'm gay."

The moment the words were out of my mouth, I regretted them. I mean, I probably shouldn't have said that to a kid who was actually stressed out enough to be in an actual stress center specifically because of how he'd been treated for being gay.

He didn't seem to mind, though. He just scoffed and shook his head. "Fuck those fuckers," he said.

I smiled. That was the exact right thing to say.

"No, seriously," he said. "They're the bullies now. The school, I mean. You know that, right?"

I hadn't thought of it that way, but in a funny way, maybe he was right. Certainly, every time I thought about the lawsuit— which was all the time these days, it was the thing that kept me awake when I lay in my hospital bed, staring at the ceiling as one staff member after another checked in on me—I had that same tight, ashamed feeling that I recognized from my days at Clarkstown.

"I guess they're just trying to win the lawsuit."

"Fuck them," he repeated.

We sat there, then, watching the water from his dramatic

spit take silently pool into a puddle on the floor. Then he added, "The fuckers."

In one of our sessions, one of the kids asked me what I did when my classmates picked on me.

"I ignored them," I said.

And then Brendan pointed out that few people ever *actually* ignore these sorts of things. "We might pretend that these things aren't happening," he said. "But in truth, even though we aren't acknowledging the events, they're causing a lot of hurt."

And I realized he was right. I hadn't been ignoring all those comments at all. I'd just been pretending that they didn't matter.

"Paige, did they hurt you?" Brendan asked.

I nodded. "Yeah."

"Does it still hurt?"

I bit my lip. I nodded ever so slightly.

"That's important to know, Paige," Brendan said. "It's real. So it's important to just accept that."

The morning of the settlement hearing came, and I was still in the stress center.

My mother called. I asked her what she thought was going to happen.

Louis stood nearby, waiting for me. We were about to go into a session about the cycle of anger.

"I think they're going to offer us a settlement," Mom said. Her voice on the other end of the phone seemed very far away.

What my mom and I wanted was for the judge to grant us a trial. If the school offered us a settlement, there would be no trial. It would just end. More than that, it would end quietly; our attorney told us that a settlement would require that we never discuss what had happened. We would take some amount of money, then never speak of it again.

I thought about Miss Ward's fake smile, about Miss Fischer's parting words: *I cannot promise to keep you safe.* I thought about all those days I was home alone while the other kids just kept going to school.

I thought about what it would feel like to take their money and then keep my mouth shut forever.

"But you're not going to take it, are you?"

There was a long pause.

"Honey," she said, "I don't know that we should keep going on with this."

"Mom," I said, and I could hear the sharpness in my own voice, a sharpness that surprised even me. "You cannot settle."

I saw two nurses look up at me. I turned my back to them and looked down. I was wearing the same pair of sweatpants I'd worn the day before. I was wearing slippers. A thought flashed through my head: *I look like a mental patient.*

And then I realized that I *was* a mental patient.

When I looked back up, Brendan had come to get Louis. Louis glanced back at me as he followed Brendan out of the room.

My mom's voice on the other end of the line was uncharacteristically quiet. "I won't settle if you don't want me to," she started. Her words were slow and deliberate, like she was afraid of upsetting me. "But you took pills, honey. You're in the stress center. I think this is too much. Maybe it's time to just let it end."

My fingers gripped the phone tightly, so tightly I could feel it all the way up in my forearm. I wanted so many things at that moment. I wanted my mother there. I wanted to cry in her arms. I wanted to return to bed, to just go to sleep and make it go away. But there was something I wanted more than all of that: I wanted to make them pay. All of them—the kids, my soccer coach, the counselors, the administrators. Every kid who had ever joked about me, and every kid who had ever laughed. I wanted to see them up on the stand. I wanted them to have to look me in the eye in a courtroom.

"Mom," I said. I was trying so hard to control my words, but I could hear the shrillness creeping into my voice, could feel my legs shaking.

I took a deep breath and started again. "Mom. If you settle . . . I swear to God . . ."

I stopped, leaned into the wall. My legs were so weak. I could feel a presence behind me, and I knew that one of the staff was standing there, standing with that ID badge around her—the badge that allowed her to come and go whenever she pleased. She was, I knew, watching me closely.

"If you settle . . ." I continued, my voice urgent now. It was hard to catch my breath. There was something hot inside me, something rising up. I looked up and saw the happy-looking WEEKLY SCHEDULE posted on the bulletin board. The letters blurred into a kind of wave. My voice sounded so tight, so angry, it didn't even sound like me. It was like the voice was coming from another animal entirely, some creature trapped deep inside my own body. A creature filled with rage.

"I will never, ever speak to you again. Do you understand?"

"Okay, honey," came my mother's voice, so far away. I imagined her alone in the kitchen. I knew she was going into the settlement hearing all alone. I knew how hard that would be for her, surrounded by lawyers. I suspected she needed me there just as much as I had needed her all this time. "Okay—"

But I couldn't hear any more. I didn't even let her finish.

"Never!" I added one more time, and I slammed the phone down in the receiver.

The schedule for the week swam before my eyes, and then I felt hot tears on my cheeks.

I was stuck here. I was just a kid. I was just some messed-up kid, and the most important thing in my life was happening somewhere else, with other people. I was stuck here inside these walls, and it was all my fault. I had done everything wrong. I had yelled at my mother when she wasn't the one I was mad at. I had hung up on her when she was only trying to help. I had taken pills when I should have known it would break her heart.

She was all alone now, and I couldn't fix any of it.

I still wasn't in control. I was a kid in sweatpants and slippers who had no control over anything, not even my own voice.

I wanted to tear all those posters off the wall. I wrapped my arms around myself and dug my fingernails into my arms hard, until tiny half moons appeared on my skin. I stayed that way for a long time, until the room stopped swimming in my tears. Then I took a deep breath, shuffled out of the room, into the hall, wiping my nose with the back of my hand.

My mother didn't settle. The days dragged on. I shuffled to pizza lunches and stroganoff dinners. I identified people I might reach out to the next time I was having a hard time: *Amber. Mariah. Erin. Maybe even Mr. Gilchrest, the nice teacher at Herron who told me about Aristotle and virtue.* I listened to Brendan talk about the importance of gratitude, of kind acts, and I read about signs of stress: *Fatigue. Nausea. Social withdrawal. Sleeplessness*—I recognized that I'd had them all. And we created a discharge plan and a home safety plan—my mother would be hiding all the knives and locking up the medicines, for one thing.

Then one day they told me I was ready to go home. Whatever "ready" looked like.

On the morning I left, Louis stood in my doorway. He had fresh scratches on his arm, and the pink marks stood out against his dark skin. When I asked him about it, he shrugged.

"I guess I have a while to go."

We weren't supposed to exchange numbers, but I wrote down his number anyway. We hugged briefly.

"Go get 'em, girl," he said. "Don't let the fuckers win, okay?"

"Yeah, okay. You either."

My mom and I were silent on the drive home. She flicked on the radio. A newscaster was talking about a Florida girl who had killed herself after months of bullying by her classmates. My mom quickly turned the news off.

I reached over and turned it on.

"Paige," my mom said in her warning/worried voice.

"What?" I asked. "You think it's going to give me ideas I wouldn't have on my own?"

I meant it as a joke, but I could see my mom cringe.

I turned the radio back on, and we heard the details: Hope Witsell, age thirteen. Good home, loving parents. Sent one explicit photo of herself to a boy she liked, and it went viral all over school, to kids at other schools. She was called names, taunted endlessly. Hung herself in her bedroom while her parents were in the house.

I turned the radio off. The streets grew more familiar outside my window.

"I won't do it again," I said quietly.

My mom kept driving, her hands on the wheel. She didn't say anything.

"Mom? Did you hear me?"

That's when I noticed her chin. It was quivering.

"I promise, Mom. I won't do it. Okay? I need you to hear that. I won't do that to you. Not again."

She took her right hand off the wheel and reached over to me. Her eyes still on the road, she grabbed me by the hand and squeezed, so tight it almost hurt.

Lila

A few weeks after I got home from the stress center, I saw Lila for the first time since I'd left Clarkstown. Erin and I had walked to Broad Ripple shopping plaza—a cozy collection of stores near a walking trail a few miles north of downtown Indianapolis. We stopped in a McDonald's for a soda.

Outside the McDonald's, in the drive-thru lane, was a small sign with both the golden arches and the words FAITH AND BLESSED. Walking toward the front door, I wondered out loud if the sign meant that that particular restaurant was blessed, or if the restaurant owner was wishing all of us faith and blessings.

I felt better. Better than I had felt in a long time.

Ethan had texted me after I got home. He must have heard about my being in the stress center, because his message said simply, *RU OK?*

I'd replied, *Yes. Thanks.*

And then, after a little bit, I sent another message.

Me: *Can I ask you something?*

Ethan: *Sure*

Me: *Do you remember when you said you didn't want people to know we were hanging out?*

Silence.

Me (after a minute): *After the cafeteria thing.*

Ethan: *Kind of.*

Me: *Did you really think that was okay?*

Silence.

I wasn't sure why I was even writing this, whether it was that

I wanted him to feel bad, or I simply wanted to understand. It was probably a little of both. Still, I needed to get it out there.

Me: *That really hurt my feelings.*

Me: *I needed a friend.*

Silence.

And then, after a minute:

Ethan: *Sorry.*

Ethan: *I'm really sorry.*

Ethan: *They were making fun of me, too.*

Me: *Who?*

Ethan: *Everyone.*

Ethan: *They kept teasing me, saying I shouldn't like you. They wouldn't stop.*

I bit my lip and looked out the window for a moment. It had never occurred to me that kids were teasing him, too, just for his association with me. And then I wrote him again.

Me: *I didn't know that.*

Ethan: *I didn't know what else to do.*

Ethan: *It wasn't cool. But I wanted them to stop.*

A long pause.

Ethan: *I'm sorry though.*

Ethan: *I really am.*

Me: *What did you say?*

Ethan: *When?*

Me: *When they teased you?*

Ethan: *I said stop, but they never did.*

Ethan: *I guess I was sick of it.*

I stared at my ceiling for a long time. My mom and I had redone my room just before I started at Herron. The pink and purple were gone. Now everything around me was a deep shade of red.

Me: *Hey.*

Me: *Thanks.*

Ethan: *For what?*

Me: *For saying sorry.*

Me: *I haven't gotten a whole lot of apologies. It means a lot.*

Me: *I feel better.*

Ethan: *Thx, Paige.*

Don't let anyone say you can't have a meaningful conversation via text. Because I was telling the truth. I did feel better. It really did mean a lot.

Now inside McDonald's, Erin and I sat in the booth, sipping our sodas. People came and went; I didn't pay much attention.

And then, I can't say why, but I felt a kind of strange energy coming from near the counter, so I looked up. And immediately, I met Lila's eye. Yasmine's sister.

If I'd ever wondered if time had softened things between us, if she felt bad about how things had turned out, the answer was in front of me. Literally, it was right there in front of me. She stared at me with hard eyes, her chin thrust forward like she'd been challenged. She was with a friend who I did not recognize; that girl, a stranger, glared at me, too.

I felt a sickening sensation spread across my stomach. I struggled to swallow the drink that was in my mouth.

"It's okay," Erin said in a low voice. "They won't do anything inside the restaurant."

My heart pounded. I picked up my drink, then placed it down again on the table. My hand was shaking.

Notice the signs of stress, the voices from the stress center came back to me. *Increased heart rate. Difficulty breathing. Trouble concentrating.*

"We'll just hang out until they're gone," Erin said. She gave me an encouraging smile, and I tried to smile back.

In the corner of my eye, I watched Lila and her friend. They took a paper bag filled with their order. They went to the drink dispenser and filled their cups. They leaned in to each other, speaking in low voices.

I became intensely aware of the smell of fried food. *Why hadn't I noticed it before?*

Another wave of nausea. I wanted to be out of that restaurant, but I didn't dare move.

Erin kept the conversation going—she leaned in to me and talked about cheerleading at Clarkstown. As an eighth grader, she had just joined the team and was telling me about some changes to the drills. She was smiling and making a point of having a good time. I forced my cheeks into a smile and nodded as she spoke. But I was barely listening. I was intensely aware of Lila, of the strange, threatening energy that I could feel—it was a thing in the room, her hatred. It had a shape and texture. I felt like I could have reached out and grabbed it, and I don't doubt for a minute that it would have seared my hand.

Then, just like that, Lila walked out the door. A moment later, we saw her behind the wheel of her dad's white car. Of course; she'd be a junior in high school now. She'd be driving.

She drove slowly, disappeared from view, then reemerged.

She was circling the restaurant. Like a predator.

"It's okay," said Erin. "She'll go home in a minute or two."

She passed by the window a few more times. Then she didn't. We waited: two minutes, five minutes, ten minutes.

"She's gone," said Erin. I breathed a sigh of relief, and I nodded.

We gathered our empty soda cups, crumpled our cardboard fries carton. We stepped back out into a beautiful evening, streaks of pink already appearing in the sky above us. We walked.

We were on the back side of the restaurant, far from the windows, when we saw Lila's father's car. It was heading toward us. Right toward us.

So many things can happen in a span of just a few seconds.

First: I understood that she was coming for me, that she had waited for me, waited stealthily out of sight, the way a hunter waits for prey.

Second: I calculated the time it would take for me and Erin to go back into the restaurant. I compared it to the distance Lila's car was from us. There was not enough time. Not nearly enough time.

Third: I thought, *This could be bad.* I didn't know what that meant exactly—what would be bad? What might happen?

The sign in front of me said FAITH AND BLESSED.

Lila slowed down.

There was no place to run, no place I could go quickly enough.

She pulled over, leaned out of the open window.

The world went into slow motion. I looked at Lila's face. It was so distorted, twisted in hate. *Animal*, I thought. *She looks animal.* She raised an arm, pulled it back behind her head. I registered that before I registered what was in it. Something flew toward me. It hit me, straight on. Hard. I felt the impact first, the rough smack of it. Then I felt everything else: Cold, ice cold. Wet. A sharp pain in my ribs. Something hit the ground. I heard the thud, the tumble of ice, laughter. Lila pulled away, tires screeching.

Her soda. It was dripping down my front. That's what had been in her hand, a twenty-ounce cup of soda, and she'd thrown it at me.

"You okay?" Erin's voice. I realized I had heard it just a moment ago, too, calling out my name. I'd been too shocked for it to register, but now I was piecing it all together. Lila had waited for me—specifically waited, for the purpose of humiliating me. She'd thrown a drink at me. Erin, dear friend, had called out to me, called out a warning, when she, too, must have been just as shocked and scared as I.

It was just a drink—just a drink thrown from inside a car. It could have been so much worse. I realized I was shaking.

"Come on," said Erin. "Let's get you cleaned up."

We walked back into restaurant, walked into the bathroom, where Erin blotted me with paper towels. I began crying then, crying hard. All these years later, and I still couldn't go out to a McDonald's in my own hometown.

Lila still hated me. She really just hated me.

She was always going to hate me.

"She's a jerk, Paige," said Erin, squeezing a rough paper towel against my shirt. "A jerk and a coward."

I nodded. I couldn't figure out why I felt so ashamed. Why was I always the one to feel ashamed?

Lila hated me simply for existing, for still being in the world at all. Lila had helped to drive me out of a school district, but not out of town, not out of this world, and I guess that infuriated her.

As Erin blotted me dry, I caught a glimpse of myself in the mirror. I was wet, but otherwise intact. I looked like me.

And that's when I realized something: Lila hated me for something she couldn't even see. I mean, my HIV was completely and totally invisible. Anyone looking at me on the street would think I was just a regular kid. They would never know—they never do know—that there's anything different about some of my cells.

And if people hate me for something that they can't even see, what chance do other kids—the ones who have things you can see—have? What about a kid who is overweight, or who has terrible acne? Who walks with a limp or, God forbid, has some sort of facial deformity? How about a kid who stutters, or whose clothes don't fit in, or who is too short or too tall, or who wears glasses, or whose skin is a different color?

What about a kid like Louis?

When you stopped to think about it, there were so many reasons that one person could choose to hate another person.

If a completely invisible virus was an excuse to turn me into an outcast, then what about all those other differences that exist between people—hair color and skin color and nose shape and body type and physical challenges and even just plain personal style? But aren't we *supposed* to be different? Aren't we always told that we should be comfortable being exactly who we are?

I was exposed to a virus before I'd even had the chance to take my first breath.

That was a fact. I couldn't change it. And if Lila hated me for my virus, then she hated me for something I couldn't control, something I could never, ever change.

Nobody could change it. The best scientists on the planet, the best doctors in the world, couldn't change it. My mother, no matter the intensity of her worrying, the fierceness of her love, couldn't change it.

HIV was part of me, and it always would be. There was nothing I could do.

I met my own eye in that McDonald's mirror. Suddenly, something about this situation seemed almost funny. Here I was in a McDonald's bathroom, blotting soda from my clothes. Lila was angry. She was filled with hate.

There would never be anything I could do about that. So there was no reason to waste my energy trying to change it.

Erin took a heap of paper towels and threw them in the trash.

She looked at me hard, then smiled slightly—the same warm smile that she'd shown to me on the day I left Clarkstown. "Are you okay, Paige?"

I nodded. I brushed a strand of hair away from my face. I realized something: my hands weren't shaking. My arms weren't shaking. My face wasn't going blank.

The voices from the stress center came back to me: *Recognize the signs of stress.*

At that moment, I recognized several things that were all jumbled up together. I recognized that I had *let* those kids get to me, had let them make me doubt myself, for something that I never could have helped, anyway. I recognized that Erin, standing there by the trash can overflowing with paper towels, was one of the most loyal, faithful friends on this planet.

I recognized *myself*—the me that liked cheese puffs and Kit Kat bars, the me that loved to dance and sing. The me that would still be there, after I had changed my clothes, after this moment had faded into the past.

I might be wet, but I was going to be able to walk out of this ladies' room, walk out of this restaurant, return to my house, with my head held high.

"Yes," I said. I looked at Erin and shrugged my shoulders. "I'm okay. I really think I am."

"You ready?" she asked.

"Yeah," I said. And I felt a lightness in my voice when I said it. "I'm ready. Let's go."

Erin and I walked out together into the warm September evening.

+ P A R T F O U R +

Becoming

Kindle

"You must be Paige!" The woman was a stranger to me, maybe thirty years old, curvy and beautiful, her dark hair pulled back into a ponytail. Her arms were spread wide, ready to embrace me, even though we were meeting for the first time.

I knew exactly who she was: Eva Payne. Her eyes were so bright I couldn't help but smile.

She wrapped her arms around me in a hug. "I'm so glad you're here."

"Hi, Eva," I said. "I'm glad to be here, too."

And I was.

I'd just arrived at Camp Kindle, Fremont, Nebraska—my first-ever sleepaway camp experience. Kindle looked just like I'd always imagined summer camp would look—wooden cabins, wide fields, dirt paths, swimming pool, duck pond. But this camp was a little different: it was specifically for children who were infected with, or otherwise affected by, HIV.

My transportation here was an Angel Flight—a private plane whose pilot volunteers to take kids to camp, or to treatment facilities. My mom had walked me to the tarmac and, as the plane lifted off, I had waved and given her the thumbs-up. I watched her get smaller and smaller until she disappeared.

The pilot and I headed upward, toward the sun, until the clouds sat below us, like piles of snow. Although I'd flown before, I'd never seen the ground like this, the wide-open view of Midwestern fields, my own country, my whole world, laid out before me.

So, I thought, *the world can look like this, too.*

From up there, the world, including my own problems, seemed very small.

Eva pulled back, held me by the shoulders, and grinned. "I am so glad you joined us, Paige."

I already knew all about Eva. When she was in college, just a twenty-one-year-old theater major at the University of Nebraska, she had seen a play about a boy with HIV. Shortly after, an idea popped into her head—one that she couldn't shake: *There should be a camp for kids who are impacted by HIV/ AIDS.* She began researching camps all over the Midwest and found nothing for kids with HIV/AIDS. There was nothing at all. She knew then: it was up to her. After relentless fund-raising, she and her merry band of volunteers chaperoned a group of fifty kids to a campsite in Nebraska.

Camp Kindle was born.

I loved this story. I loved, first of all, that even as a student, she had done something, started something, something that mattered. She hadn't waited until she was older, she hadn't waited until someone had declared her a grown-up or given her permission to make a difference. She just did it. There was something so bold about that, so confident.

Here was someone who wasn't HIV positive, whose family members weren't HIV positive, who'd had every reason in the world to ignore HIV/AIDS. But she hadn't ignored it. Instead, she had taken it on as her personal mission. She was like Dr. Cox in a way—fighting for kids who would be easier to ignore. I already loved her for that.

I watched Eva as she gave directions to the counselors, set up a registration table, scanned the camp with discerning eyes. Then we heard the rumble of a bus in the distance.

"Here come the Chicago campers!" whooped Eva.

She turned to me with a grin. "Just wait," she said. "You're going to love this."

A short while later, after a busload of kids from the Chicago area had unloaded, and car after car had pulled in and left, everyone stood around greeting one another. Kids waved to each other and hugged—many already knew each other from previous summers—and there were flurries of introductions, of shaking hands, of "Where are you from?" and "Is this your first time?" and "Which cabin are you in?"

I met one kid after another, forgetting most names almost as soon as I learned them. I knew that every kid here was either *affected* (because someone they knew and loved had HIV/ AIDS) or infected themselves, but for the most part, I couldn't tell the difference.

My heart pounded.

"Hey," said a voice next to me. "This is your first time, right?"

I turned to see a dark-haired boy, a little younger than myself, with a half-cocked, slightly mischievous grin.

I nodded. "Yeah," I said. "I'm Paige."

He held out his hand. "Nice to meet you, Paige. I'm Wallace."

Something about the way he shook my hand, like a miniature adult, and the way his mouth curled into a half smile, both mischievous and innocent, made me want to burst out laughing.

"I'm a little nervous," I confessed.

"Don't be." He grabbed the arm of a blond girl walking past him.

"Hey, you!" he said.

The girl turned and threw her arms around him. They hugged tight, for a long time, then she pulled back and smiled at me. She had a name tag around her neck: Nikki.

Nikki who is friends with Wallace, I thought, hoping I would remember her name later.

"Nikki, meet Paige," said Wallace. "Paige here is a little nervous."

"Oh, don't be," she said with a laugh. "In five minutes, everyone here will be your best friend."

"You've been here before?"

"Yeah," she said. "I've been here lots of times. It's the best."

Across the crowd, I noticed a blond boy, older than I was, surrounded by kids and counselors. Even several yards away, I noticed his startling blue eyes, his ruddy cheeks, the tiny space between his two front teeth that somehow made his smile even wider. I squinted and read his name tag: Brryan.

Brryan with two r's.

Kids kept throwing themselves into Brryan's arms and hugging him tight. Just then, Brryan looked up and winked at Nikki. Nikki stuck out her tongue at him, and he laughed.

Then she saw someone else and waved excitedly. "Hey, Cole!" She turned to me. "Hey, Cole's here."

She grabbed my arm and pulled me over to boy about my age, with shaggy hair and a wry smile. Wallace jogged after us. "Hey, wait for me," he said.

"Hey, Cole," Nikki called out. "This is Paige. Paige is coming with us to the duck pond."

"I am?" I asked.

"Sure you are," said Cole, as if it were the most obvious thing in the world.

And just like that, we were friends, heading toward the water: Nikki, Wallace, Cole, and me.

We checked into the cabins, which counselors had decorated for us—my group's was decorated with the theme "Derby

Divas," with roller skates everywhere. Then we headed back out to our first camp meeting.

Counselors taught us camp songs. The songs were goofy, childlike, but that didn't matter; everyone, even the oldest kids were singing loudly. There was nothing to do but sing along, laughing.

"They ooze in the gooze without any shoes," we sang.

"They wade in the water till their lips turn blue."

I tried not to wonder if my mom was lonely back at home. I imagined her face, imagined her knocking around the kitchen without me. I sang a little more loudly. Above me, a soft breeze rippled through trees. I was six hundred miles from home. When I looked up, Nikki was watching me. When I met her eye, she grinned, singing the whole while.

"And that's what makes a hippopotamus smile.
And that's what makes a hippopotamus smile."

I had a feeling I was going to like it here.

As the afternoon gave way to evening, Eva and another director, Michael, suggested that we might tell some of our own stories, explain what had brought us here.

"Does anyone want to volunteer to share their story?" Michael asked.

I looked around and no hands went up.

"I know that it's not easy," Michael said. "Sometimes it takes a lot of courage."

The room was still.

I could do it, I thought. *I could start.*

I tentatively raised my hand.

Michael smiled. "Paige. Thank you. Go ahead."

"Okay, well," I began. And I told them the story that had begun feeling so natural on my lips. I told them about my dad. I told them about Yasmine, about the lock-in when I told her a secret, about PAIDS and the seizures, the notes on my locker and about leaving school.

I told them how lonely I'd been.

The room was quiet as I spoke. When I finished there was just the briefest pause, one of those pauses where you can hear a pin drop. Then people applauded.

I looked out and saw Eva, nodding approvingly. She winked at me, as if to say, "Right on, girl." I grinned, and took my seat. Several people leaned over to touch me, as if to silently say, "Good job." Nikki's words came back to me: *In five minutes, everyone here will be your best friend.*

Yeah, I thought. *Yeah, I can see that.*

"Anyone else want to share?" asked Michael.

No one spoke for a few long moments. Then Brryan stood up.

"I'll go," he said. His words came out a little funny, which surprised me. Then he looked at the group. "I have some hearing loss because of some medications I've had to take. I'll speak as clearly as I can. Please bear with me."

Brryan's story began when he was just seven months old. He'd had an asthma attack, and was admitted to the same hospital where Brryan's dad worked as a lab technician. At the time, his parents were in the process of splitting up. They had been arguing about child support. Still, they had come together when their son got sick. They had sat together by Brryan's bedside, praying for their baby, for his tiny, fluid-filled lungs.

What his mother didn't know—couldn't possibly have known—was that Brryan's dad had brought to the room a syringe filled with HIV-tainted blood. He had stolen the

blood from his lab. When Brryan's mom left the room to get a
soda, his dad took the needle out. He injected the HIV-tainted
blood into his son, into Brryan.

"He didn't want to pay child support," explained Brryan
evenly. There was no malice in his voice, no anger or sorrow.
"So he tried to kill me."

Brryan's dad didn't tell anyone what he'd done. Instead, he
occasionally dropped hints, saying things like, "Why should I
pay child support when the boy's not even going to live very
long?"

Five years went by like that. For most of that time, Brryan was
a healthy, rosy-cheeked little boy. Then, almost overnight, he
became very, very sick. He dropped weight. Like my mother,
he got sick with mysterious fevers. Unlike my mother, Brryan
wasn't diagnosed until the virus had progressed to AIDS in his
body; his CD4 cells had plummeted.

The doctors gave Brryan just months to live.

"That was more than a decade ago," said Brryan.

He took a deep breath. "My father is in prison for what he
did to me, and he's due for parole in a few years. His name
is Brian Jackson. That was my name, too," said Brryan. "So
in eighth grade, I legally changed the spelling of my name. I
didn't want to carry his name anymore.

"Anyhow, that's my story. I'm still here, all these years later,
and I plan to be for a long time."

"Wow," I said under my breath as I watched him return to
his seat. "Just—wow."

Later, we stood around a campfire, roasting marshmallows.
We had to keep moving to avoid the gusts of smoke that
changed direction with tiny shifts in the evening breeze. That
was okay; it gave us a chance to meet new people. I chatted and

laughed with lots of campers, but I couldn't take my eyes off Brryan. He moved so easily, his smile was so open. I watched as he high-fived some of the older boys, chatted with Eva, laughed with other campers. I saw him bend down to talk to two seven-year-old girls, twins whom I'd noticed earlier had G-tubes, a way of feeding when AIDS makes eating too risky or difficult. I couldn't hear what he was saying, but I saw him wink at the twins; they laughed and scrambled off into the night, still smiling from their encounter with him.

He just seemed so relaxed in this world.

My own father had given me the virus, just like Brryan's dad had given it to him. But mine, at least, had not done it on purpose. And I, too, had seen some of the less flattering parts of human beings—the teasing and the name-calling. But if pressed, I could acknowledge that what I had seen came largely from ignorance.

What Brryan's dad had done wasn't ignorance: it was evil.

I couldn't quite imagine how Brryan could remain so at ease in a world in which another human being, his own father, had deliberately tried to kill him. I thought about the first time I sat in Miss Ward's office, after someone had signed my name to a note I hadn't written. I could still remember how unbearable it was to think that someone hated me.

Yet there was Brryan in front of me, just laughing and having a good time.

There was some word, some phrase, that described the thing I saw when I looked at him. The word was on the tip of my tongue, but I couldn't quite name it.

The fire crackled, sending sparks toward the sky. From across the fire, Brryan must have felt me watching. He looked up at me, met my eye, and smiled. I smiled back, then almost immediately looked down at the ground.

Wallace sidled up to me. "Hey, baby," he said. "Come here often?"

He cocked one eyebrow at me, and I laughed out loud.

It was only later that night, walking back toward the cabin, the smell of campfire still in my clothes, that I realized what word I'd been searching for, the one that described Brryan.

Forgiveness, I thought. *That's what forgiveness must look like.*

Mornings at Kindle were spent talking frankly about HIV and AIDS: how to keep ourselves healthy, how to talk about the infection with others, what was myth (*myth: you could spread it by kissing or toilet seats*) versus reality (*reality: when the time came, we'd need to practice safe sex*). Each day, more kids shared their stories—I quickly learned that Cole's mother was positive, that Nikki's brother had an AIDS diagnosis, that Wallace had been adopted as a baby, and his parents had learned only later that he was HIV positive, that there were a ton of others just like me—kids who had been born positive and just wanted to be treated like everyone else.

I learned, too, that many kids were keeping their HIV status secret from even their closest friends.

Afternoons, though, were pure fun—a release from the serious issues we'd spent the morning discussing.

The day after we arrived, for example, counselors organized the Camp Kindle Carnival. Before it began, Eva brought us to a room filled with wigs and capes and other costumes. Campers and counselors laughed as we tried on outfit after outfit—Hawaiian shirts and clown noses, Mylar wigs and sparkly sunglasses, capes and cowboy hats, tutus and sequin-covered spandex. Wallace tried on a cheerleading costume and shook pom-poms. Girls wrapped men's ties around their heads like warriors. One counselor, already wearing spangled biker shorts and ladies' sunglasses, threw a Bozo the Clown wig on his head.

All of the campers laughed and rummaged around for the silliest outfits we could find.

Outside, a face painter drew intricate patterns of butterflies, while counselors arm-wrestled with campers, dramatically letting the youngest kids win. There were games set up everywhere—water balloon tosses, sack races, competitions for carrying eggs on spoons. I rolled an apple with my nose, then went over to the Hula-Hoop competition, where I Hula-Hooped with a kid whose face was half painted as the Incredible Hulk.

"You go, Paige!" whooped Eva. She was festive in a polka-dot shirt, a polka-dot scarf, and a pink tutu over her jeans. I laughed and managed to keep the hoop circling around my hips.

A few minutes later, I was celebrating with a grape-flavored snow cone. Cole walked up to me wearing a balloon animal hat. A lollipop stuck out of his mouth. When I smiled at him, grape juice dribbled down my chin. I wiped it with the back of my hand.

"Lookin' good, Paige."

I laughed and took another slurp of my snow cone.

Nearby, a group of campers were having a pie-eating contest, planting their faces in pie tins filled with whipped cream. Nearby, two counselors—guys in sequined spandex—danced in sync. I could see Wallace walking with a stuffed pig strapped inexplicably to his baseball cap. Near them, Brryan walked stiffly; two small kids clung to each leg, one on his back. "I don't know why my shoes are so heavy today," he said as the kids fell into peals of laughter. "My shoes are just so heavy."

Anything goes, I thought. *After today, we can be anything. We can be anyone here, and still be okay.*

At that moment, I heard one counselor shout, "The degree of awesome is so high we could melt glaciers!"

I threw my arms wide and shouted to Cole, "Oh, my God, I love Camp Kindle!"

"Yeah." He nodded thoughtfully, twisting the lollipop in his mouth. He surveyed the scene around us. "Yeah. I know exactly what you mean."

That night, after running through the cabins with Nikki, singing and dancing, I lay in my bunk bed. Many of the girls around me had already fallen asleep; I listened to their breathing, and beyond the walls of the cabin, the sounds of crickets crying out into the night.

This is what it would be like, I thought. *This is what it would be like to be just a regular kid, to not be the girl with HIV. This is what it would be like to be normal, to have nothing that needed explanation, nothing that made me different from anyone else.*

I *was* a regular kid, I realized. Here, at least, at Camp Kindle, I was.

Toward the end of the week, Eva approached me. "Paige, *People* magazine would like to do a photo shoot with some campers. I was wondering if you'd like to be in it." Already, my mother and I had given permission to have my picture taken, to be one of the kids that could be used in promotional materials for the camp. *Yes*, we had said. *Yes, you can show the world that Paige Rawl goes to a camp for kids touched by HIV/AIDS.*

People magazine: I had seen it so many times, on magazine racks near the supermarket checkout counter, in so many doctors' offices. I imagined someone picking up the magazine, casually flipping through the pages the way I had so many times, and seeing my face staring out at them.

"Who else will be in it?"

"Brryan and Wallace and Anthony." Anthony was a few years younger than me, a skinny kid with large glasses. He, too, had been born with the disease.

"Yeah," I said without hesitation. "Yeah, I'll do it."

We spent the next several hours having our picture taken—Brryan wore all black, while the rest of us, the three younger campers, wore bright T-shirts. We tied Camp Kindle bandannas around us. The photographer stood us in front of a campfire for a long time but, just like on the first night, the wind kept shifting the direction of the smoke, which made us cough.

Finally, they brought us indoors and stood us against a white background, where we stood on top of a painted red ribbon; they posed the three of us so that we leaned against Brryan, all of us standing confidently with our arms crossed.

Then Brryan scooped me up, pulled me over his head, square over his shoulder and I burst out laughing. I felt as light as air.

The other two campers leaned into Brryan as he held me, and the photographer snapped away. "That's good," she said. "Yes, that's great!"

That evening, as the sun was setting, Brryan tousled my hair walking toward the campfire. "You did a good job today," he said. "It takes a lot of courage to let your HIV status be known to three and a half million people."

"Three and a half million, huh?"

He shrugged. "Just three and a half million of your closest friends." Then he grinned, his full lips crinkling into a wry smile.

There was something I wanted to ask him, but I wasn't even sure how to begin.

"Brryan," I started.

He waited.

"How . . ." I frowned. I felt like it was impossible to explain what I wanted to say. "I just . . ."

"What is it, Paige?" He stopped then, and looked at me. I loved the way he looked at me, right at me, not taking those blue eyes off of my own.

I shook my head. I didn't even know how to begin. What I wanted to ask was "How do you do it?" but even I didn't know what I meant by "it."

Somehow, Brryan seemed to know exactly what I was trying to say. He eyed me carefully, then looked down at the ground. When he looked up, he was deadly serious.

"I can't make myself into the kind of person he was, Paige. I can't hold that kind of hate in my heart."

In the distance, I heard the campers' voices, ringing out in song: *"They ooze in the gooze without any shoes . . ."* I could see smoke rising from the fire. Above us, the sky blazed pink and orange.

In two days we would be going home.

"But . . . how?" I asked.

He looked up at the sky for a long time, then he looked back at me and shrugged. He said simply, "You decide."

I thought about that, about the idea that maybe you could just decide. Brryan said, "That really is it. You decide to live a good life. It's all you have to do."

I nodded as if I understood, even though I didn't fully. Not yet.

"Paige," he said, looking hard at me. "You have to shine your own light. And when you do, when you shine your light, you begin to notice all these blessings around you. And you realize that *you* are blessed. And all the people that hurt you just kind of fall into your past."

I looked down and thought about that, thought about Yasmine and Lila and the PAIDS boys and Miss Fischer and Miss Ward falling backward into darkness, disappearing from sight.

The lawsuit was still going on; we still hadn't been granted a trial. It felt like it could go on forever.

But I wanted that—I wanted them to fall away.

"Paige." His voice was soft. "You've got a lot of light, you know."

He smiled at me, and I smiled back at him, and we stood that way for a little while.

I heard footsteps approaching. I turned around, and Nikki and Wallace and Cole were running toward us.

"Guys," Nikki said. "Come on, the counselors are jumping in the pool in their clothes!"

She grabbed my hand and started pulling me. I laughed, and waved at Brryan as Nikki dragged me away. He winked at me. Then Nikki and Wallace and Cole and I dashed toward the rest of the group.

Above us, the light of the sun gave way to the sparkle of a million stars, the light of a million other suns.

On our final night of camp, the counselors took their campers on a trust walk. They blindfolded us, made us walk around camp with hands on each other's shoulders. No one spoke; we just shuffled along, totally silent. Periodically, we had to stop. A counselor would take one of the campers by the hand, lead them carefully to a location where they sat down. We all waited for the counselor's return, then shuffled along until the next camper was pulled away. Without vision, my other senses were acute. I heard the birds chirping, the rustling of wind through leaves. The breezes were warm on my skin.

When it was my turn, my counselor said, "Paige, each day has the potential of being your best day. You decide what each day will bring."

You just decide.

"To kindle something is to spark a flame," she continued. "Let the flame act as a reminder to believe in possibilities. You have the power to light the fire of change. Don't wait to take action; if you see a need, fill it."

You decide to live a good life. It's all you have to do.

"We all hope for a cure and compassion for those living with this disease. We have a unique story. Being impacted by HIV does not define who we are."

Paige . . . you've got a lot of light.

The wind blew through my hair. Tomorrow at this time, I'd be home, back with my mother in our brick house, two blocks down from Clarkstown. In a few weeks, I would be back at Herron.

Almost a year had passed since I'd taken those pills. If I had succeeded on that day—if the pills had made it all go away, the way I'd wanted—I would never have been here. I never would have met Brryan or Eva or Nikki or Wallace or Cole, or the twins, or the counselors, or any of these amazing people.

My counselor was still speaking. "With that you can open your eyes."

I took my blindfold off. The light came flowing in.

"We all love you, Paige," she said.

"I love you, too," I said. "I love everyone here."

And I meant it. I really did.

. . .

Later that night, each cabin performed a dance. Wallace and Cole's cabin did a lip sync to a Justin Bieber song. About halfway through, each boy in the cabin danced out into the crowd, grabbed a girl, and sang to her. Wallace pulled me up, and Cole pulled up Nikki. We laughed as we moved toward the stage. Before us, a crowd of friends—how quickly we'd grown to be so close—cheered for us. Wallace shook his hips in a way that was so silly and so endearing. I met Nikki's eyes and we laughed.

Then the counselors did a lip sync to "Don't Stop Believin'." Halfway through, they all lifted Eva above their heads, the way Brryan had lifted me in the photo shoot. Everyone cheered—I think I cheered loudest of all. Then the rest of the night was a blur: we danced in the dark waving glow sticks above our heads. We watched a slide show with pictures from the week, tears streaming down our faces. We hugged one another tightly before we all headed back to the cabins for one final night in our bunks.

The founder of Camp Kindle, Eva Payne, and me goofing around at CK Nebraska. Camp Kindle is where I really found myself again.

. . .

The bus was scheduled to take campers away in the earliest hours of the morning. I wasn't leaving until much later that day—until a far more reasonable hour for an Angel Flight pilot—but Nikki and Wallace would be leaving with the bus, and I wanted to say good-bye. So Cole and Wallace and Nikki and I all met at the cafeteria just after 3:00 a.m., the morning that still looks like night. We stepped out into the darkness, kicked at the dirt, and promised to keep in touch.

This was the beginning of the end of something magical, and I knew it. The bus would take these kids, all of them, back to their own communities, to the lives they led before coming here. Many, I knew, would pretend they had been at a camp for regular kids—some would make up a name for it, so that nobody could look it up. They would go back to hiding who they were and what they were struggling with. They would quietly take medicine and hope that no one saw or wondered why. They would attend doctors' appointments and say things like, "I have allergies," and not tell anyone the real reason.

But I knew something else: I knew that they would hold this week inside of them. That they would carry this experience carefully inside them and would take it out when they felt alone, when they needed to remember that someone, somewhere, understood.

I knew this, because it was what I was going to do with the week, too.

When the bus finally pulled out, the counselors didn't just stand still and wave good-bye. They followed it, walked alongside it, waving the whole time. They walked and walked long past the moment when campers could still see them. They walked until its taillights were out of sight.

I walked with them, too.

Then Cole and I walked to the duck pond, the same place we'd gone just after we met. We watched the sun rise over the lake, pink clouds like cotton candy above our heads. There was still a tiny crescent of a moon, and I loved that, loved being with the sun and the moon at the same time. Cole chased the ducks, who flew away, startled, flapping their wings and calling out wildly before returning, only to be chased again. We stayed together, the two of us, aware of the ticking clock, aware and unable to change that finality.

I would have stayed there forever if I could.

A few weeks after I returned home, my mom burst through the door.

"It's here, Paige!" she cried. She waved a *People* magazine. "It's here!"

We flipped through the pages: a healthy Cobb salad recipe from a celebrity trainer. An article about a reality TV star's new bikini body. A story about Justin Bieber's new haircut. An advertisement for hair shampoo. Then there we were: Brryan and Wallace and Anthony and me. It was the photo where Brryan held me over his shoulder, the boys leaning in. In the photo, I am horizontal, and Brryan is holding my wrist and ankle, and I am touching Anthony, who is touching Brryan, who is leaning toward Wallace. I had to look closely to see whose hand belonged to whom.

The picture is titled "Heroes Among Us," with the caption, "An AIDS survivor inspires kids with HIV."

Before we had left Camp Kindle, Brryan had handed me a note. I started to take it from him, but before he let go, he said, "No, wait."

Then he opened it up and read it out loud to me.

Upon my homecoming, if anyone asks me who my hero is, I'll give a name that has truly inspired me this week. The name is Paige Rawl. She may be a short one, but never underestimate someone until you see their heart. . . . She will never be forgotten. Forever, she has a place in my heart.
Brryan Jackson
HOPE IS VITAL

When he finished, he handed it to me. I wrapped my arms around him, and we stood hugging for a long, long time.

Now here we were in *People* magazine together. I looked at Brryan's image; it looked like Brryan was smiling right at me. I grinned back.

What is most remarkable about this picture is how utterly unremarkable we look. Brryan looks strong and healthy, the rest of us like any other kids. And that's the thing: We are strong. We are healthy. We are just like anyone else; the evidence was right there on the page in front of me.

Truth be told, we look like a whole lot of fun. We look like the kind of kids I'd want to hang out with.

Moving On

In October, I turned on the television and saw a photograph of an African American boy, a little younger than myself. He had beautiful, soulful eyes, and a grin on his face like he might know how to get into a little bit of mischief.

He looked a little like Louis, actually.

I knew immediately that something terrible had happened to this boy.

I had called Louis several times, had called and texted to see how he was doing. Sometimes he texted me back, vague things like, *You know me, I'm the belle of the ball around here.* His texts always made me smile, but I remembered those scratch marks on his arms, and I worried.

The boy on television was named Jamarcus Bell. He was from Fishers, Indiana, about twenty miles from my house. I was right—something terrible had happened. He'd committed suicide, the news reporter was saying, after years of bullying. Kids had teased him since middle school. They threw metal at him during welding class, they called him names.

The report referred to him as the "boy who always smiled."

Last month, another boy in Indiana had died. Billy Lucas had also been teased for being gay. He'd had chairs pulled out from underneath him. Some kids had told him to go hang himself.

So he had. Billy hung himself from the rafters in his family's barn.

Now here was another teen gone because of bullying. He

was just like Billy Lucas, just like Hope Witsell, the girl who
was in the news when I came home from the stress center.

He was just like thousands that had come before.

A few days later, my mother got a call from our attorney.

I knew something was wrong by how still she was as she
held the receiver to her ear. When she spoke into the phone, it
was only in short bursts.

"But how could—?"

There was a long pause.

"But four out of five—

"Three instances? But there were so many—"

"But that's—"

"Okay, but what can we—?"

"And what would that—?"

"How long?"

I don't even think she said good-bye. She just hung up the
phone and looked down. I waited, but she did not speak.

"Mom?"

She did not look at me. She was extremely still.

"Mom. What is it?"

The refrigerator kicked on. Nearby, one of our neighbors
was listening to the radio; I heard the deejay's laughter ringing
out into the afternoon. She shook her head again. I noticed
how her shoulders sagged, and I sat down in a chair.

"That was the lawyer?"

She did not move.

"Will there be a trial?"

She looked up. Tears filled her eyes.

"Mom?" I spoke slowly. "Will there be a trial?"

She shook her head. I could barely hear what she said when
she finally spoke. "No."

I didn't say anything—I just let the news flow through me.

There would be no trial.

They would never take the stand.

I would never make my case in court.

My mom closed her eyes for a long time. Her only movement was to shake her head back and forth slowly. "I'm so sorry, honey."

I bit my lip so hard I tasted blood. "How?"

She shrugged. It was not a shrug of indifference. It was the kind of shrug that signaled loss of hope.

"Tell me, Mom."

"The judge said we won on four out of the five counts. But we needed to win all five."

I had known that we needed to win five points. From the start, the law had already been clear about the first two counts— that HIV is a disability under two different laws, and that kids with HIV should be able to attend school without harassment. Our case had required winning the three remaining points— that bullying occurred, that the school knew, and that the school had not taken reasonable steps to protect me. I couldn't imagine which of those points we'd lost.

"Which didn't we win?"

She threw up her hands. "I—"

"Which one, Mom?"

"They agreed there was bullying. . . ."

"And?"

"They agreed the school knew about some bullying."

I just looked at her. That meant that the judge thought the school had taken reasonable steps to protect me.

My mind started racing. Reasonable steps? They called it drama. They ignored my mom's phone calls and the notes she left. They defended Yasmine because she was a straight-A student. They told me to deny who I was.

I thought about Kyle, Michael, and Devin calling me PAIDS and laughing while I cheered. What reasonable steps had been taken in that moment? What about those messages on my online pictures? What about Lila's instant message? What about the notes we had told them about?

No AIDS at Clarkstown.

You bitch. You hoe.

What about my name on the bathroom wall, plain as day?

As far as I could tell, nobody had ever gotten more than a warning. Not once.

My mom was speaking slowly. "The judge only considered three instances of bullying. He said the school responded appropriately to all three."

My mouth felt dry, which perhaps explains why the only word I said came out in a whisper.

"Three?"

"The first incident with you and Yasmine, the one with the note someone signed your name to. The one where kids called out to Ethan in the cafeteria. And Miss Ryan's comment."

The fake note, the cafeteria, and Miss Ryan. But there were so many more.

"My nickname? PAIDS?"

She shook her head. "They didn't consider that."

"The instant messages? The online comments?"

She looked down; the shake of her head was only barely perceptible.

"And what about the notes you left? The phone calls? They didn't even call you back. That's 'reasonable'?"

She took a deep breath and spoke very softly. "Remember, honey," she said. "The school didn't remember my leaving any notes. They had no records of my phone calls. Nothing was ever documented. The judge had nothing to go on."

She looked me right in the eye then, and I understood she was telling me something about the world. She was telling me something that until that moment perhaps we'd both been too young, too naive, to fully understand. It was in that moment that I understood what I'd done wrong.

I'd been a child.

I'd been a child, and I'd gone to the adults in my life with a problem, expecting that their first priority would be to help me. I'd expected them to behave like I'd always been taught that adults would behave. I'd expected them to look out for me.

But sitting there in the quiet of our kitchen, shades drawn, I realized that I'd been wrong. I went to them needing adults. Instead, they had responded like potential defendants—then actual defendants—in a lawsuit. They protected *themselves*.

I'm sure their attorneys advised them that it was the only logical thing for them to do.

To have won this case, I would have needed to document things, needed to photocopy things, to make sure there were records of everything that had happened. To bring in witnesses.

I had needed to behave as no child would have ever thought to behave.

I knew something else, too. I knew that I had just crossed some sort of threshold. It was like I'd walked across a bridge and turned to look backward, only to find that the bridge had burned behind me. I could never go back. I would never return to a place where I believed that adults would do the right thing, that a child could count on the grown-ups in her life.

My mom would look out for me—she would look out for me forever. I had no doubt about that. But aside from her, I had to be careful. The world looked different from what

I'd imagined when I was a child. It was a whole lot more complicated.

I felt hot tears running down my cheeks. I placed my head in my hands and sobbed.

Almost instantly, I felt my mother's hand on my back, rubbing up and down. "We can appeal, you know," she said to me. "This isn't the end. We can file an appeal."

She was speaking faster now, the way she always does when she is angry or anxious. "We might have better luck outside of Indianapolis, with another judge. We know what we're up against now. We just need to insist on bringing in witnesses for some of the other events. We can prove—"

"How long?" I asked, and looked up at her. "How long would that take?"

"Well." She stopped talking. When she answered, it was quietly. "I don't know. Probably a couple of years."

A couple of years. It would go on through the end of high school. It might still be going on when I was in college.

I'd left Clarkstown behind when I was in middle school, and the lawsuit might still be going on when I was in college.

I shook my head. "No, Mom."

I couldn't do it. I couldn't take them with me that far into the future. I had given Clarkstown my middle school years, and already far too many of my high school years. They didn't deserve any more of my time. I wanted them gone.

All the people that hurt you just kind of fall away into your past.

I wanted them—all of them—firmly in my past.

My mom looked at me carefully. "Pumpkin, you don't have to—"

"No."

"Paige, do you understand that this is the only way—"

"It's not the only way."

She stopped, shook her head, confused.

"Mom, if the law says that the school handled this the right way, then somebody needs to change the law."

"What are you—"

"Right now, the law is so narrow it can't keep anyone safe." It didn't keep me safe, it sure as hell didn't keep Hope Witsell or Billy Lucas or Jamarcus Bell safe. I shrugged my shoulders. It really did seem so simple now.

"Let's help change the law," I finished.

I didn't know how anyone could do that, exactly. But I knew I wanted to help. There were so many kids out there. So many kids who had been treated so badly. You couldn't even turn on the news without hearing about them.

Mom stood up, walked to the window, and stared out of it for a long time.

"I am so angry," she said finally. "I am just so angry, I can't even see straight. I don't want them to get away with this."

"Mom?" I said. "If the law changes, then they have to change. They won't get to hide behind policy and procedure. They'll have to fix things."

She nodded, but it was a vague nod, a distracted nod. She still was not looking at me.

"I stood up for myself, Mom. Can you see that?"

Another nod, a tiny one.

When she didn't say anything, I said, "Mom, this is so much bigger than me. I wish it weren't. But it is. It's happening everywhere, and it's so bad."

I was crying again, then. "It's really just so bad."

She came back to the table and sat down. "So, no appeal?"

I thought about it, thought about the fact that this would be it, the end of the road. The lawsuit would end here. My relationship with Clarkstown would end here.

This is the way it would end—with nothing at all.

"No," I said finally. "Let's not appeal. Let's do something else instead."

"What, though?"

"I don't know," I said. They were maybe the truest words I'd ever spoken. "Not yet. But I can tell my story, and that's a start."

She took a deep breath and closed her eyes. Then we sat together in silence for a long time.

Finally, she spoke.

"Paige?"

I lifted my eyebrows.

"I'm proud of you. I'm really, really proud of you."

I met her eyes. With the tears still staining my cheeks, my heart a jumble of sorrow and disappointment and anger and hope, I smiled.

"Thanks," I said.

I was a little proud of me, too.

Part of the prom court at the end of my junior year.

Miss Teen Essence

It was the summer before my junior year at Herron, and I was onstage again. I was wearing the greatest dress—white and poufy with bold red roses all over it. The lights were bright, and the crowd was loud, and I loved it.

It had been almost two years since I'd been in the stress center, a year since I'd been to Camp Kindle for the first time. Since then, I'd been speaking more, traveling some, meeting kids and activists from around the country.

A few months before, I'd helped Herron High organize its first-ever HIV/AIDS Awareness Week. The halls had been plastered in posters. Every student, every teacher, every locker, was decked out with at least one red sticker. Kids wore them on their clothes, on their cheeks, on their foreheads. I passed one boy who had stuck them to his earlobes, like earrings. Red ribbons were everywhere.

In December, I had spoken at a Delaware youth forum in honor of World AIDS Day. I'd worn a black T-shirt that said simply HIV POSITIVE, and I'd told the audience members—all teens like myself—about my experiences.

After I spoke, I had noticed two pageant queens—one my age, the other a little older—in crowns and sashes.

I went right over to them.

"I love pageants!" I said. "I used to do a lot of them."

The older one had very dark skin and long, dark hair. She wore a sleek red dress and her sash read, MRS. ESSENCE. She extended her arms wide and I gave her a hug.

"Girl," she said, "you are just so brave. I loved what you said out there."

When we pulled back, she extended her hand. "Tamika Hall. Mrs. Essence 2010, and loving it."

The other girl, the younger one, said, "I'm Melanie Haynes, Miss Delaware Essence. You really were great."

"Tell me about your pageant," I said.

"Oh, honey, it's the best of them all," said Tamika. "Essence women are real women."

"It's true," said Melanie. "Girls come from all walks of life."

"Like what walks of life?" I asked.

"There's every kind of woman, all backgrounds, all colors."

"Last year's Ms. Essence lost a hundred pounds over two years and she talks all about how hard it was," said Tamika.

"And there are women who have been in bad relationships," said Melanie.

"We're talking *real* bad relationships," said Tamika, pointing to herself. "My platform is relationship violence, if that tells you anything."

"We're the Essence of the modern woman," said Melanie dramatically.

"We're about *inclusion*," said Tamika. "Giving a voice to every kind of woman."

She leaned in toward me. She had the most expressive eyes I'd ever seen. "And we are loads of fun," she said.

And just like that, I wanted to do it.

To compete, I flew to Kansas City. Tamika and Melanie had been absolutely right. This was the most fun pageant I'd ever been to—we'd rocked out to a soul band, we'd gone roller-skating, and I'd even tried doing the limbo on roller skates. We'd danced and laughed, and it turned out that bringing together so many different kinds of people made the whole thing that much more fun.

Now we were down to the final five in the Miss Teen Essence division. Each of us would get a question picked from a bowl.

The lights were bright. I could hear rustling in the audience.

The judge leaned in to the microphone and read my question.

"If you could write a book, what would it be called and why?"

I smiled, remembering the morning in eighth grade when the news of my bullying, the lawsuit, made the papers. I remembered the joke my mom and I kept making: *I'm front Paige news now.*

I spoke straight out into the audience. "I've been thinking about writing a book, actually. I've thought about calling it *Front Paige News.* That's a pun. My name is Paige, and I once made the front page of the newspaper, because I had been bullied in middle school. . . ."

I paused. It would be so easy to stop there. It would be so easy to just end on that note and say nothing else.

Remember, I was the kid who never wanted to rock the boat or make anyone uncomfortable. I was the good girl, the one who just wanted to fit in.

But if I could talk about my HIV onstage in any pageant, surely I could say it in this one.

And besides, maybe being good, *really* being good wasn't about fitting in and keeping quiet. Maybe being good required being a little more like Amber—foulmouthed, ready-for-a-fight Amber.

Amber, who would defend anyone, who would stand up for what was true, what was right. Maybe *being good* required standing up to what *is*, and fighting a little harder for what *could be.*

I took a deep breath. ". . . because I am affected by HIV."

There was no question that the audience understood. I swear, I literally heard gasps in the audience.

When I heard those gasps, I had an immediate urge to take my words back, to reach out and grab them and stuff them back inside me. Maybe it was too much, I thought. Maybe the pageant world just wasn't ready. I remembered when that first pageant brochure showed up in my mailbox and my mom was reluctant to let me do it. *There are things you don't know, okay?* she had said. She'd been so nervous. She had also been correct. I had been so young.

There had been so much I didn't know then.

But that's when I realized that people were clapping—just like that.

I'd said it, they'd gasped, and now they were applauding. I stepped back out of the lights, walked back to my place among the other girls.

And walking offstage, I thought, *Or maybe I'll name it Positive.*

It would be nice to say that I won. It would be nice to say that standing up there and saying it out loud—*I have HIV*—was so powerful that the judges agreed unanimously: the winner is the girl who spoke her truth tonight. Here is the first openly HIV-positive pageant queen. Here is her crown. See how she is just like everyone else?

In the end, though, I didn't win.

But I didn't exactly lose, either.

I won first runner-up. It was a national pageant, and I'd told them I had HIV, and I here I was. First runner-up.

Standing there onstage, I remembered my very first pageant, when I was standing there in my David's Bridal gown with

Heather's mom next to my own mom, both of them out there with their eyes shut and their fingers crossed.

I'd been through hell since then. I'd been to emergency rooms and stress centers and McDonald's bathrooms. I'd learned my truth.

And now I had spoken it.

Huh, I thought. *How about that?*

There was another pageant coming up—Miss Indiana High School America. Maybe, just maybe, I should enter.

Just to see.

"You Decide to Live
a Good Life"

(It's All You Have to Do)

The following summer, I saw a photo of Yasmine online. She was at a party for kids at North City High School—the high school into which Clarkstown Middle School feeds. The picture was part of someone's online photo album and I clicked through, looking at image after image. I recognized almost all the kids in the pictures; many of them were the same kids who had been so mean to me.

By this point, I had been on television several times, I'd spoken all over the country. I'd led antibullying vigils, I had attended the United States Conference on AIDS. I'd dined with celebrities and recovered drug addicts. I had been honored as one of just five HIV heroes in the country in a national competition; I had been flown to New York City, driven around in a limousine, and had my photos snapped on a red carpet outside of a downtown theater.

I would be eighteen in a month.

It had taken this long—longer, honestly, than it should have. But it had finally started happening: Clarkstown Middle School had begun fading into the distance, settling deep into my past.

And here, in these photos, were many of the kids who had

picked on me, almost adults now. I knew that they still talked about me, still laughed about me—Mariah had told me that. Just a couple of weeks before, I had gone out for ice cream and seen one of them. I saw the hardened narrow eyes, and I heard the whispers. I heard only one word inside the whisper. I heard the word *AIDS*.

To them, I supposed, I would always be—would only be— the girl with HIV.

I scrolled through the photos, clicking on one after another. The kids were in a basement, sprawled out on a sofa. They were drinking from red plastic cups, holding their drinks up to the camera. An Indiana University pennant hung above them. In their hooded sweatshirts and jeans, they blended together, almost like they were wearing uniforms.

I thought about what my own life would look like in photographs, thought about all the people I'd met since I'd been in school with these guys—the drag queens and recovered drug addicts and activists and good, earnest people who chose love over judgment. I thought about Brryan, remembered the feeling of him lifting me up during the *People* photo shoot, about Eva and Wallace and Louis and Ms. Lane.

I thought about my mom, too. Something had started to dawn on me recently—something I'd always known, but had begun understanding in a new way. Mom had HIV, just like I did. All these years, when I'd been so focused on my own journey, she'd been on her own. In fact, she'd been on two journeys—mine *and* hers. She had been there so completely for me that I had almost been able to forget that she had struggles, too.

I turned back to these images. For years, these kids had loomed so large in my memory, like they were some kind of demons that had been pursuing me, reaching out, grabbing hold of me from behind, pulling me back every time I tried to move forward. But sitting here in front of the computer, it felt as if I'd finally stopped running. I'd turned around and looked at them, looked right at them. For the first time, it was clear what they really were. They weren't demons at all. They weren't evil or monstrous or even all that scary.

They were just a bunch of kids.

They had been middle school kids when I knew them. Now, they were high school kids who had probably snuck some beer into their parents' basement in the suburbs of Indiana.

They looked, I realized with a start, almost dull.

In that instant, I was oddly grateful to them, grateful for the whole experience. Had it not been for their nicknames and laughing, for the seizures and the depression, the stress center and the desperate sorrow, I probably would have been right there with them in these pictures. That world I was looking at—the sectional sofa, the paneled walls, the carpeted basement floor—would have been the only world I knew.

My world now was so much broader than that. It was more colorful. It was infinitely more textured.

My HIV, I realized, had done something for me that I wouldn't have known to do for myself: it had given me a way out. It had taken me out of the smallness of the world I'd started in, and given me a glimpse of something bigger. It had shown me things that were far more meaningful than I might have seen otherwise. The things I'd seen were filled with heartbreak and humanity, compassion and caring.

My HIV had given me a purpose, something I might otherwise never have found.

I shouldn't have needed HIV to see these things. All those things are out there—all those amazing people with their strength and stories. They're there for anyone, for everyone. You don't need HIV, or anything in particular, to discover them. You just need a heart that's a little bit open, a head that's ever so slightly curious.

But would I have discovered them on my own? Or would I have been just another kid without a purpose, surrounded by people who were exactly like me, dismissing anyone— everyone—who was different?

Would I have thought that my little world *was* the world?

I clicked off the pictures, shut down the computer, and walked away. I already knew the answer.

And I was grateful.

Graduating high school in June 2013. The storm had passed.
I felt happy and confident, and I knew I could accomplish
great things. All I had to do . . . was go and do it!

. . .

One month before I was crowned Miss Indiana High School America—openly, with my HIV simply a fact—an honor roll student at a religious school went to a party in Steubenville, Ohio. The girl was younger than I was at the time. At the party, she got drunk. Boys who were supposedly her friends raped her, peed on her, and otherwise mistreated her. Pictures of the event were circulated all over the internet, sometimes with comments like, "Some people deserve to be peed on." The case made national news; eventually, two football players were convicted in the attack.

But similar cases, elsewhere, were playing out differently. In Canada, a teenage girl was gang-raped at a party; her classmates circulated photographs of the event. After that, she was harassed and taunted, called a slut by friends and strangers alike. SLUTS AREN'T WELCOME HERE, said one note. She received numerous propositions for sex. Former friends turned their backs on her, called her names in the street.

The girl had been a straight-A student with a goofy sense of humor. After months of being bullied, she killed herself. Later, people left notes on a website her family established in her memory, commenting that she deserved to die.

In California, yet another girl who was gang-raped at a party killed herself after being bullied online about the event.

In Minnesota, a thirteen-year-old girl—a girl who had never even kissed a boy—killed herself after being called a slut and a prostitute by classmates.

A twelve-year-old boy in New York killed himself after having been teased for his height, and for the fact that his father had died when he was just four years old.

A thirteen-year-old California boy shot himself after having been bullied for being gay.

The stories go on and on. Suicide is the third-leading cause of death in young people—and at least one study suggests that half of those suicides are related to bullying. You can find a thousand stories online—a thousand kids, born with hope, happy for some period of their lives, and dead today because people in their lives chose cruelty instead of kindness.

What struck me most about those stories was the way people turned against the victims—kids who had never done anything wrong in the first place. Their biggest crimes were having been raped, being pretty or not pretty or autistic or having a health condition or being gay or simply being themselves. I thought about some of those messages I got once upon a time—*You look like an AIDS baby mama. You bitch. You hoe.* I am far enough away from having received those messages that they no longer feel as personal—but they aren't so far away that I can't remember what it felt like to be on the receiving end of them.

What is this thing we do, I wonder, this all-too-common human tendency to attack other people, or to pile on to attacks? Why do we choose to shame people, mob style, for who they are? Or worse, for something bad that happened to them, something they never even did wrong in the first place? Are we so convinced that our world is just, that it's fair, that we can be sure that people are always, somehow, to blame for everything bad that strikes them? Is there no such thing as bad luck?

Or, maybe it's the opposite. Maybe we are so afraid of bad luck that we punish those who have it—punish them ruthlessly—as a defense against any bad luck that might strike us. Or maybe we're at once so tribal, and so insecure, that we only know that we're inside a group by pushing someone else outside.

Or, who knows, perhaps it all comes down to this: humans are afraid of what they don't understand. And we are at our absolute worst when we are afraid.

I don't know. I don't expect I'll ever know.

I just know it has to stop.

. . .

On April 3, 2013, I testified before the Indiana Senate on behalf of House Bill 1423, an antibullying law. I testified along with the mothers of several Indiana children who, because they were bullied, no longer walk this earth.

The bill defines bullying as anything that creates a hostile learning environment for a student—whether it happens in school or out, whether it seems trivial to an administrator or not. It requires every public school to develop bullying prevention programs. It mandates reporting of bullying, and requires that teachers and administrators are trained in the best ways to address bullying.

On April 10, 2013, that bill became law.

That's a good start. I'm glad we're demanding that schools do more than just create a bullying policy. I'm glad we're asking them to really get in there, to document, to intervene, to stand up for every one of their students exactly the way a child would hope adults would.

But it's just a start. There's something else that needs to happen—something that kids, too, can do.

I speak to school groups all the time and I hear stories. I hear stories of kids who feel different. I'm telling you: all of them feel isolated in their differences. And I know exactly what that's like—God knows, when I was in middle school, I was so aware of my own struggle, it was almost all I could see.

But now that I hear these stories, I keep thinking. And now, as I talk, there is always this thought in the back of my mind: what if our differences could be the thing that brings us together?

Think about that.

What if, instead of feeling isolated in the thing that makes us different—I have *this* rare thing, you have *that* rare thing, each of us in our own world—we joined forces? I mean all of us—every one of us who has ever felt different, for any reason.

Imagine a gathering—an actual gathering of real people. People show up, tentatively at first, just a few brave stragglers, asking, "May I come in?"

The answer is yes. You, who are taller than your peers, and you who are shorter. Come in. You, who lost a parent, and you, whose parent is different from any other parent you know. You, the kid who once made an embarrassing mistake in front of your peers, and you, who lies awake at night paralyzed by the fear of making any mistake. All of you: join us.

Imagine people are coming faster now, there is a steady stream, everybody carrying the thing that makes them stand apart. You with the funny ears, you who speaks loudly, you who can't hear, and you who struggles to understand math. You who can't sit still in class, you who doesn't look like what a boy or girl is supposed to, you who weighs more than your peers, you who weighs less. All of you. Come. Let's just decide that the very fact that we stand out, that we all feel different, is enough to bring us together.

If we can let ourselves, all of us, be united by the simple fact of having a difference, we will be bigger and stronger and more powerful than anyone who might otherwise make us feel small.

And you know what? We'll have more fun, too. We will be the world's most colorful block party.

Recently, for the first time, there was a Miss America contestant who was openly autistic. Another had Tourette's syndrome. Another modeled a bikini while hobbling on crutches. And yet another was open about the fact that she was about to get a double mastectomy—both her breasts removed—as a preventative measure against the breast cancer that killed her mother, her grandmother, and her great-aunt.

Who knows? Maybe a pageant queen with HIV really isn't that remarkable after all.

I got to visit the Seventeen *magazine offices in New York when I was chosen as a finalist in their 2013 Pretty Amazing Contest.*

. . .

This past summer I went to Camp Kindle, this time as a counselor, and I met a fellow counselor. Andrew was on my team during counselor Color Wars. He was an aspiring orthopedic surgeon, attending a premedical program in Nebraska. He loved country music. He had never known anyone with HIV or AIDS, but like Eva Payne, found himself drawn to these kids. We were both counselors for the youngest kids in camp—he for the boys and I for the girls. I watched him with campers, and I was struck by how easily he laughed, how quick he was to wrap an arm around a kid who was down, to lift a child onto his back, piggyback style.

I told him about my own story, and he did not pity me. He simply listened.

During one of the staff meetings, he and some other counselors said they wanted to put me up into a cheer stunt. I told them how to place their arms, how to bend their knees, then lift and throw. I flew through the air, then came back to earth and felt his arms catch me.

And that may have been the moment I realized something else: he was pretty darned cute, too.

When I got back to Indianapolis, my mom noticed how often he and I talked on the phone.

"Do you like him?" she asked.

I smiled and didn't say anything.

"Paige?" she said. "Does he like you?"

I closed my eyes and when I opened them, I couldn't help it. I beamed. "Mom, he's awesome."

"Does he have goals?" she asked.

"Yeah, Mom, he's got a great head on his shoulders."

"And he's a good guy?"

"The best."

She shook her head. "Oh, my God, Paige. The look on your face."

"You should see him with the kids," I said. Just thinking about that made me feel happy. "I don't know, Mom. I think maybe I met my Prince Charming."

Not too long after that, Andrew visited me at college. My mom called me up and said, "Do I get to meet him when he's here?"

"Yeah, Mom. I'll bring him for dinner."

Mom cooked us steak fillets and twice-baked potatoes, and she even convinced me to sing a country song or two. He didn't know I could sing, so we broke out the karaoke machine, and I belted out Carrie Underwood. A look of surprise came over his face. I laughed. I looked at them sitting together—my goofy mother, still up for everything, and this amazing young man, my Prince Charming, with whom I was completely and totally in love.

Visiting the Ball State University Dance Marathon
back in 2011. I got to be involved with the planning,
and I found the college I wanted to attend after graduation!

. . .

As I write this, I'm just beginning college. I started Ball State University this fall, where I'm helping organize the annual Dance Marathon, which raises money for Riley Hospital. I'm working directly with Riley families, which is pretty great, being a Riley kid myself. I'm planning to study molecular biology; my career goals have changed from wanting to be Dr. Cox to wanting to discover the medicines she prescribes. There's much talk now about the next generation of HIV drugs—maybe someday even an HIV vaccine. During the time I wrote this book, a baby born HIV positive in Jackson, Mississippi, was reported to have been "cured" of the infection, an incident that sparked a large multisite clinical trial. Meanwhile, there is some optimism that an HIV vaccine might be less than a decade away. I would love to be on the front line, being a part of the team that makes HIV a thing of the past. I want to create a vaccine for those who aren't infected—and to make life with HIV totally indistinguishable from life without HIV, for those who have already been infected.

There's more work to be done; a few weeks after I learned about the baby in Jackson, the state senate in Kansas—a Midwestern state not unlike my own state of Indiana—passed a bill that would allow the quarantine of people with HIV/ AIDS. All these years later, fear of disease can still win over information.

Catching up with Dr. Martin Kleiman, who treated both me and Ryan White—one of the first and most influential pediatric AIDS patients—at Indiana University's Dance Marathon.

I know this: I will continue to work with HIV children in some capacity. Perhaps to them, I'll seem as adult as Dr. Cox always seemed to me—so mature, like someone who has it all together. Maybe I will tell one of those children about my own experiences growing up with HIV.

Maybe the child I'm working with won't entirely understand what I am saying. Perhaps she will struggle to connect the world that I describe with her own world, the one that *is*. Maybe when I'm done talking, she will smile at me—such a real and genuine smile it will crack my heart in two.

"It's not that way anymore," she'll say with a shrug. And I'll know, in that simple shrug, that it's true: in this new world, her world, cruelty to anyone with HIV, maybe even HIV—or who knows, maybe even cruelty itself—is finally a thing of the past.

Here's hoping.

And I do, I really do: I hope.

My mom is my biggest supporter. Here we are before a Masquerade Ball in 2008.

When I was a kid, I wanted to be Dr. Cox
when I grew up. She's still one of my heroes.

Afterword

It was other people who saved me. When my journey was at its most difficult, when I was most isolated from peers, when I tried in all the worst ways to escape my loneliness, it was the people who stood by me that saved me.

The little moments with them mattered most: Singing along to a song on the radio together. Making faces in the mirror. Styling our hair in ridiculous ways and laughing late into the night. Sharing a bag of cheese puffs. All of that endless talk about clothes and boys and television shows.

They made me feel normal, just like any other kid.

If you, reading this, are in the middle of your own darkness, hold tight. Your own people are out there—those friends who will love you for exactly who you are. When you find them, you'll laugh harder than you ever imagined. That laughter will fill all the nooks and crannies of your heart, all those places where pain had been.

And you'll find them if you hang on. So hang on.

If you're lucky enough to not understand what it's like to be surrounded by darkness, I'm telling you: someone near you needs kindness. They need it today. They need it desperately. Offer it. Sit with them awhile. Ask them questions. Get to know them. Then get to know them better. Share a bag of cheese puffs.

It really is that easy.

Finally, if you're an adult and there are kids in your care who are telling you something, please listen. Don't say there's nothing you can do. Don't say "kids will be kids." Don't shrug your shoulders, and please, please don't call it "drama."

It is hard to be a child in the presence of an adult. It takes strength to go to the grown-ups in your life. It takes courage to ask for that help.

Honor that. If you're not sure what to do, ask someone. Do your homework. Listen.

Don't ever stop trying.

I didn't plan this journey, and I certainly wouldn't have chosen it. But the things that happened made me who I am. They're inside me now, part of me, in the same way a tiny virus has always been a part of me.

I'm stronger today because of it. I have a voice I didn't before. That's a gift—a gift I can use to make the present-day world a little kinder.

I hope you'll join me in that.

It's a complicated and sometimes sad and seriously beautiful world we live in. There's plenty of work to be done.

And you know what? We're all in it together.

I know now that I was given this life because I am strong enough to survive it. And when the darkness cleared, I wanted to use my experience to make a difference for others. If you are in the darkness now, hold on. I promise, you can do it. You can get through all the negativity and live a life that is positive.

Acknowledgments

Ali Benjamin, my cowriter—There's not enough words I could say about you. Thank you for all of the long hours you have put into helping me share my story. It is greatly appreciated! I couldn't have done this without you and I can't thank you enough for all that you've done. There's no one else I would have rather shared this journey with.

To Kristen Pettit, Jen Klonsky, and the rest of the team at HarperCollins and to Mollie Glick at Foundry Literary + Media—Thank you for all you have done to help me share my story. I truly couldn't have picked a better team to work with!

Aunt Kim and Uncle Randy—Thanks for being there for my mom and me since the beginning of our diagnoses and standing by our sides through it all. I love you bunches!

Candi—You're the best sister anyone could ever have, I love you. I'm proud of the wonderful mother you are and thank you for blessing me with three beautiful nieces.

Mammal—Thank you for being my biggest fan. I love you.

Mark—You've truly been a father figure in my life, thank you for everything.

Jay Asher—It is such an honor to be introduced by an author who has inspired so many through the book *Thirteen Reasons Why*. Thank you for all that you are doing for those who have been a victim of bullying!

Eva Payne—Thank you for treating me like one of your own and for Camp Kindle, a place that has totally changed my life.

Riley Hospital for Children—To the doctors, nurses, and lab technicians who have taken care of me since my diagnosis, thank you! I can't imagine having been treated anywhere else.

Herron High School administration and faculty—Thank you for allowing me to be myself, supporting me, and for all the wonderful memories. I will always be grateful!

Thank you to those of you who have stood by me when a lot of others wouldn't during some of my toughest times.

Help and Resources

Consider making a donation to make a better world.

If you want to help other children who are facing health issues, and/or who are specifically affected by HIV/AIDS, please consider making a donation to two of my favorite charities:

Camp Kindle

This camp, for children and teens whose lives are touched by HIV/AIDS, was profoundly important to me. The experience is 100 percent free of charge to all campers . . . and it's life changing. By helping send a child to camp, you will transform lives. Visit www.campkindle.org/donate.html.

Riley Children's Foundation

I have been a patient at the Riley's Ryan White Infectious Disease Center since being diagnosed HIV positive in 1997. The Riley team has always provided outstanding medical care in a loving, supportive environment . . . and they never turn a child away, regardless of the family's ability to pay. Donations ensure that Riley continues to provide first-rate care to all children. To donate, visit www.rileykids.org.

I assure you that your contribution will help shape a better world.

HIV FACTS

What is HIV?

HIV is the infection that causes AIDS.

H—Human—This particular virus can only infect humans.

I—Immunodeficiency—HIV weakens your immune system by destroying cells that fight disease and infection.

V—Virus—A virus takes over cells one at a time in the body of its host.

What is AIDS?

AIDS is a disease of the immune system characterized by a weakened ability to fight infections.

A—Acquired—AIDS is not something you can contract; you acquire it after a certain point in your HIV status.

I—Immuno—Your immune system includes all the cells and organs needed to fight off disease or infection.

D—Deficiency—You reach an AIDS diagnosis when your immune system is "deficient," or weakened, from the HIV infection. HIV becomes AIDS when your CD4 count—a measurement of the amount of healthy immune cells in a drop of blood—falls below two hundred.

S—Syndrome—A collection of symptoms. AIDS is a syndrome, not just a single disease.

How is HIV spread?
- Through four bodily fluids only:
  — Blood
  — Semen
  — Vaginal fluids
  — Breast milk

- Through unprotected sexual intercourse (vaginal, anal, or oral) with someone who has HIV or AIDS
- Mother-to-child transmission during pregnancy, childbirth, or breastfeeding if the mother has HIV or AIDS
- Sharing needles or syringes with someone who has HIV or AIDS

How is it not spread?

You cannot get HIV/AIDS from:

- Shaking hands with someone who is infected
- Hugging, kissing, or otherwise touching someone who is infected
- Sharing water fountains, drinking glasses, plates, or utensils with someone who is infected
- Eating food prepared by someone who is infected
- Toilet seats
- Swimming pools or hot tubs
- The air
- Getting sneezed or coughed on by someone who is infected
- Insect bites

HIV Statistics

- As of 2009, it is estimated that there are 1.5 million adults and children living with HIV/AIDS in North America, excluding Central America and the Caribbean.
- 26,000 people in North America (again, excluding Central America and the Caribbean) die from AIDS every year.
- One in six people living with HIV in the United States are **unaware** of their infection.
- An estimated fifty thousand new HIV infections occur in the United States each year.

- An estimated one in four new HIV infections is among **youth ages thirteen to twenty-four**.
- Every 9.5 minutes someone in the United States contracts HIV.

Treatments

There is no cure for HIV/AIDS, but treatment is available. If you have been exposed to HIV, or worry that you might have been exposed, get tested. Do not wait. There are many great medicines that help people live well with the disease—and the sooner you start taking them, the better they'll work.

Where to Get an HIV Test in Your Area

In the United States, go to http://hivtest.cdc.gov. Just type in your zip code and find places near you. In Canada, the Canadian AIDS Society (listing on the following page) has hotlines that will help you find HIV testing.

HIV/AIDS RESOURCES

There are many fantastic organizations working to improve the lives of people with HIV/AIDS and to prevent new HIV/AIDS infections. Some organizations are focused on international efforts to stop the HIV/AIDS epidemic. Others provide support services or access to health care. Still others provide other support services—emotional support, a sense of community, education/information, testing, and more.

Some of these organizations are listed below, and the information about them is accurate as of June 16, 2014. Please note that none of the following organizations has endorsed or is otherwise affiliated with me, my story, or this book.

United States: AIDS.gov

This website offers HIV/AIDS information from the federal government. You'll find prevention, testing, treatment, and research information, as well as links to other sources of information. www.aids.gov

AIDS Service Organization Finder

Nearly all communities in the United States have support services for those with HIV/AIDS. To find service organizations in your area, simply type in your zip code and the distance you are willing to travel. You can even sort by the type of service you need—including legal services, testing and counseling, financial assistance, case management, and education. www.asofinder.com

Camp Kindle

Free summer camp programs for children who are infected with, or otherwise affected by, HIV/AIDS. Open to children ages seven through fifteen. There's a Camp Kindle West (in California) and a Camp Kindle Midwest (in Nebraska). Both provide a refuge from the challenges of living with HIV and a supportive environment where children find growth, acceptance, and education. www.campkindle.org

Planned Parenthood

Planned Parenthood is the leading provider of women's sexual and reproductive health services in the United States. They offer affordable health care for women and teens, including HIV testing, and they provide education and information about women's health. One in five women in the United States has visited a Planned Parenthood health center at least once in her life. www.plannedparenthood.org

Canadian AIDS Society

The Canadian AIDS Society has set up toll-free phone lines in each province and territory that you can call to get answers to your questions about HIV and AIDS and arrange to get tested. www.cdnaids.ca/hotlinesandsupport

BULLYING FACTS

Types of Bullying

Bullying is an act of **repeated** aggressive behavior that seeks to intentionally hurt another person—physically or mentally.

Physical—Any form of physical attack. Damage or taking someone's belongings may also count as physical bullying.

Verbal—name-calling, insulting, teasing, or offensive remarks

Indirect—spreading rumors about someone, exclusion from a group, or sending abusive mail

Cyberbullying—any type of bullying that is through electronic medium, like texts, phone calls, email, instant messaging, sending unwanted pictures, videos, or bullying on websites

None of these types of bullying are acceptable. None are "harmless." Don't stand for it, and don't stand idly by when you see it.

Bullying Statistics: United States

• This year, **over thirteen million** American kids will be bullied or cyberbullied.

• It is estimated that 160,000 children miss school every day due to fear of attack or intimidation by other students.

- One in five teens who are bullied or cyberbullied think about suicide. One in ten actually attempt suicide.
- Youth who are bullied are **twice as likely** to commit suicide as those who are not bullied.
- One out of every ten students who drop out of school do so because of **repeated** bullying.
- Every seven minutes a child is bullied.
- One study showed that although 70 percent of teachers believe they "almost always" intervene when their students are being bullied, only 25 percent of students thought this was actually the case.
- 64 percent of children who are bullied do not report it.

It's not just the United States, either. A 2010 research project studying thirty-three Toronto junior high and high schools reported that 49.5 percent of students surveyed had been bullied online.

Canadian teachers ranked cyberbullying as their issue of highest concern out of six listed options—89 percent said bullying and violence are serious problems in our public schools.

Canada ranked twenty-sixth and twenty-seventh out of thirty-five countries on measures of bullying and victimization, according to a recent World Health Organization survey.

If you are bullied
- You can stand up for yourself by calmly telling the bully to stop, but don't fight back on their level—this won't help and it might make the situation worse.
- Don't isolate yourself. Tell someone. Talk to an adult that you trust. If that person doesn't respond, or doesn't respond

swiftly enough, talk to someone else. Keep a record of the incidents to share with teachers, administrators, and parents.

• Don't simply accept it as something that cannot change, and do not let it change how you feel about yourself. Do not let the bullies win. You matter.

If you see someone else getting bullied

• Most bullying doesn't happen when adults are watching. But it does occur in the presence of other kids. If you see someone getting bullied, do not stand by and watch; instead, stand up and say something. Calmly and firmly tell the bully that their behavior isn't okay—that it's not funny, harmless, or acceptable.

• Some research suggests half of all bullying will end if a bystander decides to intervene.

• If you don't feel like you can safely stand up to a bully, get help from a trusted teacher or other adult. If the bullying includes threats—or if you have reason to believe someone is at risk of being hurt, be sure to tell an adult right away.

• Reach out and be kind to the person being bullied. Encourage them to seek help. Remind them they don't deserve to be bullied. Simply knowing someone is on their side can make a big difference.

National Hotlines

The National Suicide Prevention Lifeline
1-800-273-TALK (8255)

If you or someone you know is in suicidal crisis or emotional distress, please call.

The call is free and available twenty-four hours a day. Your call will be routed to the crisis center nearest to you.

Boys Town National Hotline
1-800-448-3000

A twenty-four-hour, toll-free, confidential hotline staffed by specially trained counselors.

Teens, parents, and others can get help with bullying, abuse, anger, depression, school issues, and more.

BULLYING RESOURCES

There are many, many fantastic organizations working to stop bullying, with great resources. Here are a few I especially like:

The Bully Project
A movement inspired by the terrific documentary *Bully*, the Bully Project offers tool kits for educators, parents, and students—including tips on what to do if you need help, and where to turn. You can also share stories, learn about antibullying projects in your area, and even start your own. www.thebullyproject.com

Stopbullying.gov
A federal website maintained by the Department of Health and Human Resources, this site explores what bullying and cyberbullying means, offers tips for stopping bullying, and allows you to explore your state's laws about bullying.

The It Gets Better Project
A collection of videos and resources reminding LGBT youth around the world, many of whom hide their sexuality due to fear of bullying, that they are not alone, and that life gets better. Includes over fifty thousand videos from LGBT allies. www.itgetsbetter.org

The Olweus Bullying Prevention Program

Olweus is a proven approach to antibullying that schools can use. It integrates school-wide, individual, classroom, and community aspects that collectively create a positive and safe school environment in K–12 schools. www.clemson.edu/olweus

Stop Bullying: Speak Up

A program of the Cartoon Network, this site lists kid-friendly videos, tips, games, and resources. www.cartoonnetwork.com/promos/stopbullying

Do Something

The country's largest nonprofit for young people and social change, with 2.5 million members. Their antibullying program includes a text-based "Choose Your Own Adventure"–style game that shows the steps you can take to reduce bullying. www.dosomething.org

National Bullying Prevention Center of the PACER Center

The PACER Center advocates for needs of children with disabilities, but their bullying prevention resources are helpful to all. On this website, you'll find thoughtful resources like tip sheets for kids, educator tool kits, videos, shared stories, and more. www.pacer.org/bullying

In Canada: Kids Help Phone
1-800-668-6868

A free, anonymous, and confidential phone and online professional counseling service for youth. Big or small concerns. 24/7. 365 days a year.